Pit Boss Wood Pellet

Grill & Smoker Cookbook

for Beginners

A Complete Grilling guide with Simple and Delicious Outdoor Grill
Recipes to Grill, Sear, Bake, Roast and Smoke
(Full Color Edition)

Shawn Stone

TABLE OF CONTENT

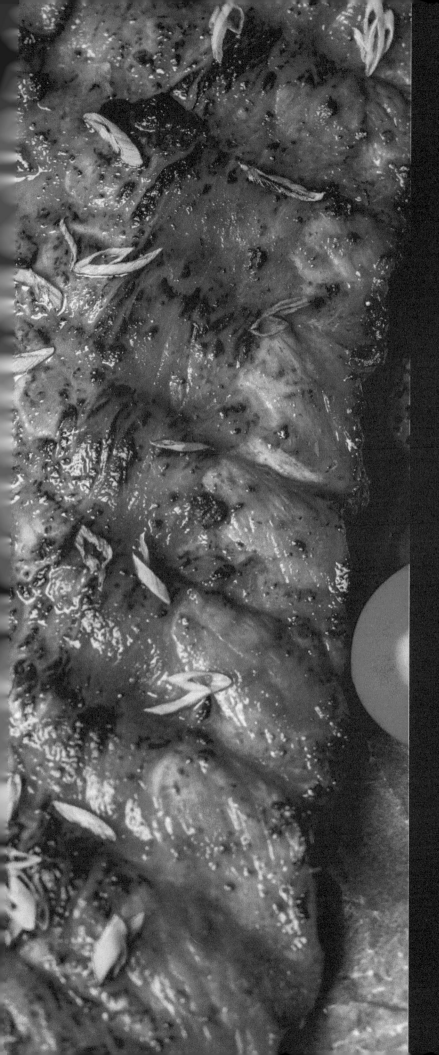

INTRODUCTION

Welcome to a thrilling journey through the art of pellet grilling, a journey that transformed my culinary landscape ever since the Pit Boss Wood Pellet Grill became the centerpiece of my backyard. This cookbook is an ode to that transformation - a collection of recipes that unlock the full potential of pellet grilling, each dish a testament to the flavors and adventures the Pit Boss has brought into my life.

My love affair with the Pit Boss began on a whim, driven by curiosity and a longstanding passion for outdoor cooking. What I didn't anticipate was how this grill would revolutionize the way I cook. With its impeccable control and versatility, the Pit Boss allows me to smoke, grill, roast, and even bake with unparalleled ease. Its ability to maintain precise temperatures means I can trust it with my most intricate recipes, and the wood pellets infuse a delectable smoky flavor that can't be replicated with gas or charcoal.

This cookbook goes beyond mere recipes; it's a guide to embracing the simplicity and satisfaction of cooking with a Pit Boss. From slow-smoked barbecue classics to quick and delightful grilled treats, each page is filled with flavors influenced by the natural woodiness of pellets. Whether you're a seasoned grill master or a newcomer to the smoke-infused world, these recipes will inspire you to explore the robust capabilities of your Pit Boss.

So, ignite your pellets, set your temperatures, and prepare to delight in the aromas and tastes that only a Pit Boss Wood Pellet Grill can deliver. Together, let's turn every meal into an occasion worth celebrating.

CHAPTER 1:

Pit Boss Wood Pellet Grill 101

The Pit Boss Wood Pellet Grill is a compact yet robust grill, designed for those who seek the flavor of wood-fired cooking without requiring extensive space. It fits comfortably on small patios or balconies, making it an ideal choice for urban dwellers or those with limited outdoor areas. Despite its smaller footprint, the Pit Boss Wood Pellet Grill offers ample cooking space with a main cooking area and an additional upper rack. This setup is perfect for simultaneously grilling and smoking, allowing you to prepare a diverse range of dishes from steaks to vegetables and even baked goods.

Equipped with a digital control board, the Pit Boss Wood Pellet Grill makes it easy to set and maintain precise temperatures, ensuring consistent cooking results whether you're looking to slow smoke ribs or sear a juicy burger. The ability to adjust temperatures from 180 to 500 degrees Fahrenheit allows for a versatile cooking experience, catering to a wide array of dishes and preferences. The porcelain-coated cooking grids are another highlight, providing a non-stick surface that not only helps in easy food release but also simplifies cleaning and maintenance.

The grill's pellet hopper, although compact, holds enough pellets to sustain several hours of cooking, accommodating extended smoking sessions without the need for frequent refills. Mobility is another key feature, with two large wheels that facilitate easy movement around your cooking space or into storage. Sturdily built with steel and coated with a high-temperature powder finish, the Pit Boss Grill is designed to withstand the elements and provide years of reliable grilling.

Overall, the Pit Boss Wood Pellet Grill stands out for its practical design, ease of use, and the exceptional flavor it brings to the table. It's a fantastic choice for those new to pellet grilling as well as seasoned grill masters looking for a dependable, space-efficient model. Whether it's a quiet family dinner or a small backyard gathering, this grill is equipped to handle it all, ensuring delicious results with minimal hassle.

Pellet grilling represents a blend of modern convenience and traditional flavor, making it a favorite among those who appreciate the authenticity of wood-fired cooking without the hassle commonly associated with traditional grills. The Pit Boss Wood Pellet Grill exemplifies this by utilizing compressed hardwood pellets, which are both the fuel and the flavor source, streamlining the grilling process with both efficiency and ease.

What are Wood Pellets?

Wood pellets are small, cylindrical pieces made from compressed sawdust. They are produced from various types of wood, each imparting a unique flavor to the food. These pellets are designed to burn clean and hot, producing minimal ash, making them environmentally friendly and easy to clean up.

How Pellets Work in the Grill

In the Pit Boss Wood Pellet Grill, pellets are stored in a hopper and then automatically fed into a fire pot under the grill by an auger. This system is controlled by the digital settings on the grill, allowing you to adjust the rate at which the pellets are fed into the fire and thus control the cooking temperature. As the pellets burn, they produce smoke, which imparts that desirable, smoky flavor to the food.

Advantages of Using Wood Pellets

Wood pellets provide exceptional temperature control and consistency, enabling precise heat adjustments without frequent manual intervention thanks to the grill's automated feeding system. This ease of use, combined with the pellets' ability to produce a rich, smoky flavor, enhances the versatility of the grill for a variety of cooking methods including grilling, smoking, and

baking. Moreover, pellets burn cleanly and efficiently, generating minimal ash and making cleanup simple and straightforward.

Understanding these basics of pellet grilling will enhance your cooking experience, making it not only enjoyable but also producing consistently delicious results. Whether you're a seasoned chef or a casual weekend griller, the Pit Boss Wood Pellet Grill, powered by high-quality wood pellets, brings simplicity, control and flavor to your outdoor cooking adventures.

The Pit Boss Wood Pellet Grill stands as a paradigm of modern outdoor cooking, bringing together the authenticity of traditional grilling with the precision of modern technology. This grill is renowned for its ability to perform a wide range of cooking methods - from grilling and smoking to baking and roasting - all with an ease that is hard to find in other grills. The features and benefits are as follows:

- **Versatility:** One of the most compelling features of the Pit Boss Wood Pellet Grill is its versatility. It allows you to explore various cooking styles with just one device. Whether you're looking to sear steaks at high temperatures, slow smoke a rack of ribs, or even bake a pizza, the Pit Boss handles it all. This versatility makes it an all-in-one solution for any cooking enthusiast.

- **Precision Temperature Control:** Equipped with an advanced digital control board, the Pit Boss Grill offers precise temperature settings that can be easily adjusted to suit the needs of different dishes. The control board maintains the temperature consistently, which is crucial for achieving perfect results every

time, particularly for dishes that require long cooking times at steady temperatures.

- **Convenience:** The use of wood pellets not only offers a cleaner operation by minimizing ash production but also simplifies the cooking process. The automatic pellet feeding system ensures a steady flow of pellets to maintain the desired temperature without the need for constant manual intervention, which is often necessary with traditional charcoal grills.

- **Flavor:** The use of natural hardwood pellets also contributes to the distinct flavor profile of the food. Unlike gas grills, the Pit Boss imparts a smoky flavor that is characteristic of traditional wood cooking. The choice of pellet variety - from hickory and mesquite to apple and cherry - allows for flavor customization, enhancing the gastronomic experience.

- **Efficient Design:** The grill's design is both robust and efficient, featuring a durable construction that stands up to various weather conditions, ensuring longevity and durability. The internal components are designed to maximize heat retention and distribution, ensuring efficient cooking and reduced pellet consumption.

- **Ease of Maintenance:** Cleaning and maintaining the Pit Boss Grill is straightforward thanks to its design and the ash management system. Regular cleaning is simplified, which not only makes the grill more enjoyable to use but also extends its lifespan.

The Pit Boss Wood Pellet Grill is not just a cooking device but a gateway to exploring the rich flavors and techniques of outdoor cooking. Its user-friendly features and efficient design make it a favorite among both novices and seasoned grill masters alike.

Guide on Setting up Pit Boss Grill

Setting up your Pit Boss Wood Pellet Grill is a straightforward process that paves the way for countless enjoyable grilling experiences. Here's a step-by-step guide to help you get started with your new grill:

1. UNBOXING AND ASSEMBLY
- Check All Parts: Upon unboxing your Pit Boss Grill, ensure all parts are accounted for as per the manual's inventory list. This check prevents any surprises during assembly if a piece is missing or damaged.
- Assembly: Follow the detailed instructions provided in the manual. This will typically involve attaching the legs, setting up the main barrel, and fitting the pellet

hopper and cooking surfaces. Tools needed for this assembly are usually basic, such as screwdrivers and wrenches, which are sometimes included with the grill.

2. PLACEMENT
- Selecting the Location: Choose a safe, stable surface for your grill. It should be outdoors in a well-ventilated area, away from any combustible materials. Ensure the grill is on level ground to avoid any operational issues.
- Protection: If possible, place the grill under a cover or in a slightly shaded area to protect it from extreme weather conditions. However, make sure the location still complies with safety guidelines for open flames.

3. INITIAL INSPECTION AND HOOKUPS
- Connections Check: Inspect the grill for any loose parts or connections, especially around the hopper and the auger system, which feeds the pellets into the firepot.
- Electricity Supply: If your model includes electronic controls or an ignition system, ensure it is near an electrical outlet or has a safe extension cord to power it.

4. ADDING PELLETS
- Filling the Hopper: Load the hopper with quality wood pellets. Choose the flavor based on the type of food you plan to cook and the taste profile you desire.
- Prime the Auger: Before the first use, it's important to prime the auger system. Turn on the grill and set it to smoke, allowing it to run until you see pellets fall into the firepot. This ensures the system is fully loaded with pellets for the initial ignition.

5. INITIAL BURN-OFF

- Burn-Off Process: Set the grill to a medium-high temperature (around 350°F to 400°F) and let it run for about 30-40 minutes. This process burns off any residue from manufacturing, such as oils or dust, and is crucial for food safety and taste quality on your first cook.

6. SAFETY CHECKS

- Final Walkthrough: Review all steps to ensure everything is assembled correctly and all systems are functioning. Check the grill's stability on the ground and make sure no parts are loose.
- Review Safety Features: Familiarize yourself with the grill's safety features, such as emergency shut-off or temperature controls, as outlined in the manual.

By carefully following these setup instructions, your Pit Boss Wood Pellet Grill will be ready for its first use. Always refer to the specific instructions and safety warnings provided by the manufacturer in the grill's manual, as details may vary slightly between models and manufacturing periods.

Using the Controls

Mastering the controls of your Pit Boss Wood Pellet Grill is essential for getting the most out of your grilling experience. The grill features a digital control board that simplifies the cooking process, allowing you to maintain precise temperatures and make adjustments as needed easily. Here's a guide to help you understand and effectively use the controls on your Pit Boss Grill:

Understanding the Digital Control Panel

The digital control panel is the command center of your Pit Boss Grill. It typically includes several key components:

- **Power Button:** This button turns your grill on and off. Pressing the power button will initiate the start-up sequence or shut down the grill, depending on its current state.

- **Temperature Control Dial:** This dial allows you to

set the cooking temperature. Temperatures on Pit Boss grills can usually range from as low as 180°F to as high as 500°F. Some models might include specific settings for smoking, roasting, or grilling.

- **LCD Display:** This display shows the current temperature inside the grill. It may also show the set temperature or other important information, depending on your model's features.

- **Meat Probe Input:** If your model includes a meat probe, there will be a port on the control panel to plug it in. The meat probe allows you to monitor the internal temperature of your food without opening the lid and disturbing the cooking environment.

- **'P' Setting Button:** On some models, this button adjusts the pellet feed rate in the "Smoke" mode, affecting the temperature and amount of smoke produced. This is useful for low and slow cooking where precise control over smoke and heat is crucial.

How to Use the Controls
✧ STARTING UP YOUR GRILL:

Ensure the hopper is filled with pellets.
Plug in the grill and turn it on using the power button.
Set your desired temperature using the temperature control dial. The grill will begin the ignition process, and you'll see the temperature start to rise on the LCD display.

✧ USING THE MEAT PROBE:

Insert the meat probe into your food and connect it to the probe input on the control panel.
The internal temperature of your food will be displayed on the LCD screen, allowing you to cook your food to the perfect temperature.

✧ ADJUSTING THE 'P' SETTING (IF APPLICABLE):

For models with this feature, you can adjust the 'P' setting to increase or decrease the smoke output. This is particularly useful when you're aiming for a specific flavor or texture on your smoked meats.
Experiment with different 'P' settings to find what works best for the types of food you are cooking.

✧ MONITORING AND ADJUSTING TEMPERATURE:

Keep an eye on the LCD display to monitor the grill's temperature.
Adjust the temperature as needed by turning the temperature control dial. This flexibility allows you to sear steaks at high temperatures or maintain a low temperature for extended smoking periods.

SHUTTING DOWN:

Once you've finished cooking, turn the dial to the off position.
Depending on your model, the grill may enter a cooldown cycle where the fan runs to burn off excess pellets and cool the grill safely.

By familiarizing yourself with the digital control board on your Pit Boss Wood Pellet Grill, you can take full advantage of its capabilities, leading to better grilling results and more enjoyable cooking experiences. Whether you're a seasoned grill master or new to the world of pellet grilling, these controls offer the precision and ease needed to cook delicious, perfectly grilled meals.

Advanced Techniques

Advanced techniques on your Pit Boss Wood Pellet Grill can elevate your grilling game and expand the variety of dishes you can create. Here's how to leverage some of the advanced cooking methods that your grill makes possible:

Low and Slow Smoking

Smoking is an art that requires patience and precision, and your Pit Boss Grill is excellently equipped for this task with its ability to maintain low temperatures over extended periods.

✓ Setting the Temperature: For most smoking applications, set your grill to maintain a temperature between 225°F and 275°F. These temperatures are ideal for breaking down the connective tissues in tougher cuts like brisket or pork shoulder, rendering them tender and flavorful.
✓ Wood Pellet Choice: The type of pellets you use can significantly influence the flavor of your smoked meats. Hickory and mesquite impart a strong, smoky flavor, while apple and cherry provide a milder, sweeter note.
✓ Managing Smoke: Use the 'P' setting on your grill to adjust the smoke intensity. Higher 'P' settings increase the amount of smoke by modifying the pellet feed rate and fan speed, which can be great for adding extra smokiness to your meats.
✓ Meat Preparation: Apply a rub or marinade to your meat well in advance to enhance its flavor. For best results, allow the meat to sit with the rub overnight in the refrigerator.
✓ Using a Meat Probe: Always use a meat probe to monitor the internal temperature of your meats. This is crucial to ensure that they reach the safe and desired doneness without the need to frequently open the grill and disrupt the smoking process.

Searing

Searing meat on a pellet grill can achieve that delicious crust often associated with high-temperature grilling.

✓ High Heat: Preheat your grill to the highest temperature setting, usually around 450°F to 500°F. This high heat is necessary to create a Maillard reaction, which develops the rich, caramelized crust.
✓ Direct Heat: If your model has a sear zone or a direct flame access, use it to expose the meat directly to the flames, enhancing the sear.
✓ Prep the Grates: Ensure the grates are clean and apply a light coat of oil to prevent sticking and to aid in the searing process.
✓ Quick Sear: Place the steaks or other meats directly over the hottest part of the grill. Sear each side for a few minutes only, just enough to form a crust. Avoid moving the meat around too much as it sears.

Baking and Roasting

Your Pit Boss Grill can function like a convection oven, which is perfect for baking pizzas, bread, or even desserts.

✓ Even Heat: Set your grill to the recommended temperature for baking or roasting. The convection-like movement of hot air inside the grill chamber ensures even cooking.
✓ Use the Right Cookware: Use cast iron or other grill-safe bakeware that can withstand high temperatures. Ensure that air can circulate around the pan for even cooking.
✓ Monitoring: Keep a closer eye on the food as cooking times may be slightly different from a traditional oven. Utilize an oven thermometer to verify the grill's temperature if necessary.

These methods will help you achieve excellent results every time, whether you're smoking a pork shoulder, searing a steak, or baking a batch of cookies. These advanced techniques will help ensure you impress your guests with your grilling prowess.

Maintenance Tips

Maintaining your Pit Boss Wood Pellet Grill is crucial for ensuring it operates efficiently and lasts for many grilling seasons. Regular care not only helps in preserving the quality of your grill but also enhances your cooking experience by ensuring consistent performance. Here are some essential maintenance tips to keep your Pit Boss Grill in top condition:

Cleaning

1. After Every Use:
Grates: Once the grill cools down, brush off any food residue from the grates using a grill brush. For a deeper clean, you can occasionally wash the grates with warm soapy water, rinse, and thoroughly dry before replacing them.
Grease Management System: Empty the grease tray and clean it with soapy water. Check and clean the grease bucket if your grill includes one. Ensure that all paths for grease runoff are clear and unobstructed to prevent flare-ups and unwanted smoke.

2. Every Few Uses:
Interior Cleaning: Vacuum out ash and debris from inside the grill, focusing on the fire pot, burn grate, and the lower cooking chamber. Ash buildup can impede airflow and affect temperature control.
Inspect and Clean the Burn Pot: The burn pot should be checked for pellet ash and clumps, which should be removed to maintain proper airflow and efficient burning.

3. Seasonal Maintenance:
Deep Cleaning: At least once a season, give your grill a thorough cleaning. Remove all internal components and vacuum the interior. Wash the cooking chambers with a mild detergent, rinse well, and let dry completely.
Check for Rust: Inspect the grill for any signs of rust or corrosion, especially if you've noticed any discoloration or paint chipping. Treat rust spots early to prevent them from spreading, using a grill-safe rust remover or converter.

Maintenance Schedule

1. Pre and Post Season:
Gaskets and Seals: Check the condition of any gaskets or seals around the grill lid and replace them if they are

worn or damaged to keep the grill efficient and minimize smoke leakage.
Hinges and Latches: Lubricate hinges and latches with a food-safe lubricant to ensure they operate smoothly.

2. Check and Tighten Hardware:
Periodically check all screws, bolts, and fasteners to ensure they are tight and secure. Vibration from regular use can loosen these components over time.

Troubleshooting Common Issues

1. Temperature Fluctuations:
If you notice unstable temperatures, make sure the pellet hopper is full and the auger is feeding pellets smoothly. Check for pellet dust or debris that might be causing a blockage.
Ensure the temperature sensor is clean and unobstructed.

2. Excessive Smoke or Poor Combustion:
Examine the burn pot for excessive ash build-up, which can restrict airflow and affect combustion quality.
Check that the fan is working correctly and that the air intake and exhaust are clear from obstructions.

3. Grill Not Igniting:
Ensure the igniter is functioning properly. It may need cleaning or, if defective, replacement.
Check that the pellets are reaching the burn pot and that the pellet type is appropriate for your grill.

Regular maintenance and proper cleaning are key to the longevity and performance of your Pit Boss Wood Pellet Grill. By adhering to these maintenance tips, you'll ensure your grill remains in prime condition, ready for whatever grilling challenge you throw its way.

Chapter 2: Beef

Seared Peppercorn Beef Steak

🕐 *PREP TIME: **10** MINUTES, COOK TIME: **8** MINUTES, SERVES: **4***

🍴 **INGREDIENTS:**
- 4 beef ribeye steaks
- 2 tbsps. cracked black pepper
- 1 tbsp. kosher salt
- 2 tbsps. olive oil
- Mesquite wood pellets

♨ **DIRECTIONS:**
1. Preheat your Pit Boss Grill to 450°F with the flame broiler open.
2. Rub the steaks with olive oil, then season with salt and cracked black pepper.
3. Place the steaks on the grill and sear directly over the flame for 3-4 minutes per side for medium-rare, or until desired doneness.
4. Let the steaks rest for 5 minutes before serving. Serve hot.

Roasted Beef Tenderloin with Cherry Tomatoes

🕐 *PREP TIME: **15** MINUTES, COOK TIME: **40** MINUTES, SERVES: **4***

🍴 **INGREDIENTS:**
- 1 whole beef tenderloin (2-3 pounds)
- 1 pint cherry tomatoes
- ¼ cup olive oil
- 2 tbsps. fresh rosemary, chopped
- 2 tbsps. fresh thyme, chopped
- 3 cloves garlic, minced
- 1 tsp. kosher salt
- 1 tsp. black pepper
- Pecan wood pellets

♨ **DIRECTIONS:**
1. Preheat your Pit Boss Grill to 400°F.
2. In a small bowl, mix olive oil, rosemary, thyme, garlic, salt, and pepper.
3. Rub the beef tenderloin with half of the olive oil mixture.
4. Place the tenderloin on the grill and grill for about 20 minutes.
5. Toss cherry tomatoes with the remaining olive oil mixture. Place the cherry tomatoes on the grill next to the tenderloin.
6. Continue cooking for another 20 minutes, or until the internal temperature of the tenderloin reaches 135°F for medium-rare and the cherry tomatoes are tender and slightly blistered.
7. Let the tenderloin rest for 10 minutes before slicing. Serve the sliced tenderloin with the roasted cherry tomatoes.

Slow-Roasted Beef Chuck Roast

🕐 *PREP TIME: **20** MINUTES, COOK TIME: **8** HOURS, SERVES: **6***

🍸 **INGREDIENTS:**
- 1 beef chuck roast (4-5 pounds)
- 2 tbsps. kosher salt
- 2 tbsps. black pepper
- 2 tbsps. garlic powder
- 2 tbsps. onion powder
- 1 cup beef broth
- Oak wood pellets

🍳 **DIRECTIONS:**
1. Preheat your Pit Boss Grill to 250°F.
2. Combine salt, pepper, garlic powder, and onion powder. Rub the roast thoroughly with the spice mix.
3. Place the chuck roast on the grill.
4. Insert a meat probe into the thickest part of the roast.
5. Smoke at 250°F for about 4 hours, or until the internal temperature reaches 165°F.
6. Wrap the roast in aluminum foil, pour the beef broth inside, and return it to the grill.
7. Continue smoking for 4 hours until the internal temperature reaches 205°F.
8. Let the roast rest for at least 1 hour before slicing. Serve warm.

Classic Grilled Beef Burgers

🕐 *PREP TIME: **10** MINUTES, COOK TIME: **14** MINUTES, SERVES: **4***

🍸 **INGREDIENTS:**
- 2 pounds ground beef
- 1 tbsp. kosher salt
- 1 tbsp. black pepper
- 1 tbsp. garlic powder
- 4 burger buns
- Your favorite burger toppings (lettuce, tomato, cheese, pickles, etc.)
- Mesquite wood pellets

🍳 **DIRECTIONS:**
1. Preheat your Pit Boss Grill to 450°F with the flame broiler open.
2. In a bowl, mix ground beef, salt, black pepper, and garlic powder. Form into 4 patties.
3. Place the patties on the grill.
4. Grill directly over the flame for about 5-7 minutes per side, or until the internal temperature reaches 160°F.
5. Toast the burger buns on the grill for the last 1-2 minutes of cooking.
6. Assemble the burgers with your favorite toppings and serve warm.

Coffee-Rubbed Beef Flank Steak

⏱ PREP TIME: **15** MINUTES, COOK TIME: **16** MINUTES, SERVES: **4**

🍸 INGREDIENTS:
- 1 beef flank steak (about 2 pounds)
- 2 tbsps. ground coffee
- 1 tbsp. brown sugar
- 1 tsp. kosher salt
- 1 tsp. black pepper
- 1 tsp. paprika
- ½ tsp. cayenne pepper
- Cherry wood pellets

😋 DIRECTIONS:
1. Preheat your Pit Boss Grill to 400°F.
2. In a small bowl, mix ground coffee, brown sugar, salt, black pepper, paprika, and cayenne pepper.
3. Rub the spice mixture all over the flank steak.
4. Place the steak on the grill and grill for 6-8 minutes per side, or until the internal temperature reaches 135°F for medium-rare.
5. Let the steak rest for 10 minutes before slicing against the grain. Serve warm.

Spicy Beef Sausages

⏱ PREP TIME: **10** MINUTES, COOK TIME: **20** MINUTES, SERVES: **4**

🍸 INGREDIENTS:
- 8 beef sausages
- 2 tbsps. olive oil
- 1 tbsp. smoked paprika
- 1 tsp. cayenne pepper
- 1 tsp. garlic powder
- 1 tsp. onion powder
- 1 tsp. kosher salt
- Hickory wood pellets

😋 DIRECTIONS:
1. Preheat your Pit Boss Grill to 400°F.
2. In a small bowl, mix olive oil, smoked paprika, cayenne pepper, garlic powder, onion powder, and salt.
3. Brush the sausages with the spice mixture.
4. Place the sausages on the grill.
5. Grill for about 20 minutes, turning occasionally, until the sausages are cooked through.
6. Serve warm.

Beer-Braised Beef Short Ribs

🕐 *PREP TIME: **20** MINUTES, COOK TIME: **6** HOURS, SERVES: **4***

🍸 **INGREDIENTS:**
- 3 pounds beef short ribs
- 2 tbsps. kosher salt
- 2 tbsps. black pepper
- 1 onion, chopped
- 2 cloves garlic, minced
- 1 bottle dark beer
- 2 cups beef broth
- Thyme wood pellets

🍳 **DIRECTIONS:**
1. Preheat your Pit Boss Grill to 250°F.
2. Season the short ribs with salt and pepper.
3. Place the short ribs on the grill and smoke for 3 hours.
4. In a large Dutch oven, combine the onion, garlic, beer, and beef broth. Add the short ribs to the Dutch oven.
5. Place the Dutch oven on the grill and braise the short ribs for an additional 3 hours, or until tender.
6. Serve warm with the braising liquid as a sauce.

Smoked Beef Brisket Delight

🕐 *PREP TIME: **15** MINUTES, COOK TIME: **10** HOURS, SERVES: **6***

🍸 **INGREDIENTS:**
- 1 whole beef brisket (5-6 pounds)
- 2 tbsps. kosher salt
- 2 tbsps. black pepper
- 2 tbsps. garlic powder
- 2 tbsps. onion powder
- 1 cup beef broth
- Hickory wood pellets

🍳 **DIRECTIONS:**
1. Preheat your Pit Boss Grill to 225°F.
2. Mix salt, pepper, garlic powder, and onion powder. Rub the brisket thoroughly with the spice mix.
3. Place the brisket on the grill, fat side up.
4. Insert a meat probe into the thickest part of the brisket.
5. Smoke at 225°F for about 6 hours, or until the internal temperature reaches 165°F.
6. Wrap the brisket in butcher paper or aluminum foil and pour the beef broth inside.
7. Return the brisket to the grill and continue smoking for 4 hours, until the internal temperature reaches 205°F.
8. Let the brisket rest for at least 1 hour before slicing. Serve warm.

Italian Beef Meatloaf

🕐 *PREP TIME: **15** MINUTES, COOK TIME: **1** HOUR, SERVES: **6***

🍴 **INGREDIENTS:**
- 2 pounds ground beef
- 1 cup breadcrumbs
- ½ cup grated Parmesan cheese
- 2 eggs
- ¼ cup milk
- 1 small onion, finely chopped
- 2 cloves garlic, minced
- 1 tbsp. Italian seasoning
- 1 tsp. kosher salt
- 1 tsp. black pepper
- ½ cup marinara sauce
- Oak wood pellets

🍳 **DIRECTIONS:**
1. Preheat your Pit Boss Grill to 350°F.
2. In a large bowl, mix ground beef, breadcrumbs, Parmesan cheese, eggs, milk, onion, garlic, Italian seasoning, salt, and pepper. Form into a loaf shape.
3. Place the meatloaf on a baking sheet lined with parchment paper.
4. Place the baking sheet on the grill and bake for about 1 hour, or until the internal temperature reaches 160°F.
5. During the last 10 minutes of cooking, brush the top of the meatloaf with marinara sauce.
6. Let the meatloaf rest for 10 minutes before slicing. Serve warm.

Honey Garlic Beef Tenderloin

🕐 *PREP TIME: **15** MINUTES, COOK TIME: **40** MINUTES, SERVES: **4***

🍴 **INGREDIENTS:**
- 1 whole beef tenderloin (2-3 pounds)
- ¼ cup honey
- 2 tbsps. soy sauce
- 2 tbsps. olive oil
- 4 cloves garlic, minced
- 1 tsp. black pepper
- Cherry wood pellets

🍳 **DIRECTIONS:**
1. Preheat your Pit Boss Grill to 400°F.
2. In a small bowl, mix honey, soy sauce, olive oil, garlic, and black pepper.
3. Rub the beef tenderloin with the honey garlic mixture.
4. Place the tenderloin on the grill and grill for about 30-40 minutes, turning occasionally, until the internal temperature reaches 135°F for medium-rare.
5. Let the tenderloin rest for 10 minutes before slicing. Serve warm.

Maple-Glazed Beef Meatballs

🕐 PREP TIME: **15** MINUTES, COOK TIME: **20** MINUTES, SERVES: **4**

🍸 INGREDIENTS:
- 2 pounds ground beef
- 1 cup breadcrumbs
- ½ cup grated Parmesan cheese
- 2 eggs
- 2 tbsps. minced garlic
- 1 tbsp. Italian seasoning
- 1 tsp. kosher salt
- 1 tsp. black pepper
- ½ cup maple syrup
- ¼ cup soy sauce
- Maple wood pellets

🍴 DIRECTIONS:
1. Preheat your Pit Boss Grill to 400°F.
2. In a large bowl, mix ground beef, breadcrumbs, Parmesan cheese, eggs, garlic, Italian seasoning, salt, and pepper. Form into meatballs.
3. Place the meatballs on the grill.
4. Grill for about 15-20 minutes, turning occasionally, until the meatballs are cooked through.
5. In a small bowl, mix maple syrup and soy sauce. Brush the glaze over the meatballs during the last 5 minutes of cooking.
6. Serve warm.

Southwest Beef Stuffed Peppers

🕐 PREP TIME: **20** MINUTES, COOK TIME: **40** MINUTES, SERVES: **4**

🍸 INGREDIENTS:
- 4 bell peppers, tops cut off and seeds removed
- 1 pound ground beef
- 1 cup cooked rice
- 1 cup black beans, drained and rinsed
- 1 cup corn kernels
- 1 cup shredded cheddar cheese
- ½ cup salsa
- 1 tsp. chili powder
- 1 tsp. cumin
- 1 tsp. kosher salt
- 1 tsp. black pepper
- Mesquite wood pellets

🍴 DIRECTIONS:
1. Preheat your Pit Boss Grill to 400°F.
2. In a large bowl, mix ground beef, rice, black beans, corn, ½ cup cheddar cheese, salsa, chili powder, cumin, salt, and pepper.
3. Stuff the bell peppers with the beef mixture.
4. Place the stuffed peppers on the grill and cook for about 35-40 minutes, or until the peppers are tender and the beef is cooked through.
5. During the last 5 minutes of cooking, sprinkle the remaining cheddar cheese on top of the peppers.
6. Serve warm.

Korean BBQ Beef Short Ribs

🕐 *PREP TIME: 20 MINUTES, PLUS 30 MINUTES FOR MARINATING, COOK TIME: 6 HOURS, SERVES: 4*

🏆 **INGREDIENTS:**
- 3 pounds beef short ribs
- ¼ cup soy sauce
- 2 tbsps. brown sugar
- 2 tbsps. sesame oil
- 4 cloves garlic, minced
- 1 tbsp. grated ginger
- 1 tsp. black pepper
- Sesame seeds for garnish
- Apple wood pellets

🍳 **DIRECTIONS:**
1. Preheat your Pit Boss Grill to 250°F.
2. In a large bowl, mix soy sauce, brown sugar, sesame oil, garlic, ginger, and black pepper.
3. Add the beef short ribs to the bowl and marinate for at least 30 minutes.
4. Place the short ribs on the grill and smoke for 3 hours.
5. Wrap the ribs in aluminum foil and continue cooking for another 3 hours, or until tender.
6. Garnish with sesame seeds before serving. Serve warm.

Caribbean Jerk Beef Kebabs

🕐 *PREP TIME: 20 MINUTES, COOK TIME: 12 MINUTES, SERVES: 4*

🏆 **INGREDIENTS:**
- 2 pounds beef sirloin, cut into cubes
- 1 red bell pepper, cut into chunks
- 1 green bell pepper, cut into chunks
- 1 red onion, cut into chunks
- 2 tbsps. olive oil
- 2 tbsps. jerk seasoning
- 1 tbsp. soy sauce
- 1 tbsp. lime juice
- Pecan wood pellets

🍳 **DIRECTIONS:**
1. Preheat your Pit Boss Grill to 450°F with the flame broiler open.
2. In a large bowl, mix olive oil, jerk seasoning, soy sauce, and lime juice.
3. Add the beef, bell peppers, and onion to the bowl and toss to coat evenly.
4. Thread the beef and vegetables onto skewers.
5. Place the skewers on the grill and grill directly over the flame for about 10-12 minutes, turning occasionally, until the beef is cooked to your desired doneness.
6. Serve warm.

Chapter 3: Pork

Smoky Pork Carnitas

🕐 *PREP TIME: **20** MINUTES, COOK TIME: **8** HOURS, SERVES: **6***

🍸 **INGREDIENTS:**

- 4 pounds pork shoulder, cut into chunks
- 2 tbsps. kosher salt
- 2 tbsps. black pepper
- 1 tbsp. cumin
- 1 tbsp. chili powder
- 1 tbsp. oregano
- 4 cloves garlic, minced
- 1 onion, chopped
- 1 cup orange juice
- 1 cup chicken broth
- Mesquite wood pellets

🍴 **DIRECTIONS:**

1. Preheat your Pit Boss Grill to 250°F.
2. Season the pork shoulder chunks with salt, pepper, cumin, chili powder, and oregano.
3. Place the pork shoulder, garlic, onion, orange juice, and chicken broth in a disposable aluminum pan.
4. Place the pan on the grill and smoke for about 6 hours, or until the pork is tender and easily shredded.
5. Remove the pork from the pan, shred it, and spread it out on a baking sheet.
6. Increase the grill temperature to 450°F and cook the shredded pork directly on the grill for 10-15 minutes, until the edges are crispy.
7. Serve warm in tortillas with your favorite toppings.

Tangy BBQ Pork Ribs

🕐 *PREP TIME: **20** MINUTES, COOK TIME: **6** HOURS, SERVES: **6***

🍸 **INGREDIENTS:**

- 3 racks pork ribs
- ¼ cup kosher salt
- ¼ cup black pepper
- ¼ cup paprika
- 2 tbsps. garlic powder
- 2 tbsps. onion powder
- 1 cup apple cider vinegar
- 1 cup BBQ sauce
- Hickory wood pellets

🍴 **DIRECTIONS:**

1. Preheat your Pit Boss Grill to 250°F.
2. Combine salt, pepper, paprika, garlic powder, and onion powder. Rub the ribs thoroughly with the spice mix.
3. Place the ribs on the grill and smoke at 250°F for 3 hours.
4. After 3 hours, wrap the ribs in aluminum foil and pour apple cider vinegar inside. Continue cooking for another 2 hours.
5. Unwrap the ribs, brush with BBQ sauce, and cook for an additional hour, unwrapped, until the sauce sets.
6. Serve warm with extra BBQ sauce on the side.

Herb-Rubbed Pork Loin Roast

🕐 *PREP TIME: **15** MINUTES, COOK TIME: **1.5** HOURS, SERVES: **6***

🍴 **INGREDIENTS:**
- 1 pork loin roast (about 3-4 pounds)
- 2 tbsps. fresh rosemary, chopped
- 2 tbsps. fresh thyme, chopped
- 4 cloves garlic, minced
- ¼ cup olive oil
- 1 tsp. kosher salt
- 1 tsp. black pepper
- Cherry wood pellets

🍳 **DIRECTIONS:**
1. Preheat your Pit Boss Grill to 350°F.
2. In a small bowl, mix rosemary, thyme, garlic, olive oil, salt, and pepper.
3. Rub the pork loin roast with the herb mixture.
4. Place the pork loin roast on the grill and roast for about 1.5 hours, or until the internal temperature reaches 145°F.
5. Let the roast rest for 10 minutes before slicing. Serve warm.

Spicy Pork and Pineapple Skewers

🕐 *PREP TIME: **20** MINUTES, COOK TIME: **12** MINUTES, SERVES: **4***

🍴 **INGREDIENTS:**
- 2 pounds pork loin, cut into cubes
- 1 pineapple, cut into chunks
- 1 red bell pepper, cut into chunks
- ¼ cup soy sauce
- 2 tbsps. sriracha
- 2 tbsps. honey
- 2 cloves garlic, minced
- 1 tbsp. olive oil
- Pecan wood pellets

🍳 **DIRECTIONS:**
1. Preheat your Pit Boss Grill to 450°F with the flame broiler open.
2. In a large bowl, mix soy sauce, sriracha, honey, garlic, and olive oil.
3. Add the pork, pineapple, and bell pepper to the bowl and toss to coat evenly.
4. Thread the pork, pineapple, and bell pepper onto skewers.
5. Grill the skewers directly over the flame for 10-12 minutes, turning occasionally, until the pork is cooked to your desired doneness.
6. Serve warm.

Maple Bourbon Glazed Pork Belly

🕐 *PREP TIME: **20** MINUTES, COOK TIME: **4.5** HOURS, SERVES: **6***

🍸 **INGREDIENTS:**
- 3 pounds pork belly
- ½ cup maple syrup
- ¼ cup bourbon
- 2 tbsps. soy sauce
- 2 cloves garlic, minced
- 1 tsp. black pepper
- 1 tsp. kosher salt
- Hickory wood pellets

🍽 **DIRECTIONS:**
1. Preheat your Pit Boss Grill to 250°F.
2. In a small bowl, mix maple syrup, bourbon, soy sauce, garlic, black pepper, and salt.
3. Rub the pork belly with the glaze mixture.
4. Place the pork belly on the grill and smoke at 250°F for about 4 hours.
5. Increase the grill temperature to 450°F and grill for an additional 20-30 minutes, basting with the remaining glaze every 10 minutes, until the pork belly is crispy.
6. Let the pork belly rest for 10 minutes before slicing. Serve warm.

Sweet and Spicy Pork Tenderloin

🕐 *PREP TIME: **15** MINUTES, COOK TIME: **1** HOUR, SERVES: **4***

🍸 **INGREDIENTS:**
- 1 pork tenderloin (about 2 pounds)
- ¼ cup honey
- 2 tbsps. sriracha
- 2 tbsps. soy sauce
- 1 tbsp. olive oil
- 3 cloves garlic, minced
- 1 tsp. black pepper
- Apple wood pellets

🍽 **DIRECTIONS:**
1. Preheat your Pit Boss Grill to 350°F.
2. In a small bowl, mix honey, sriracha, soy sauce, olive oil, garlic, and black pepper.
3. Rub the pork tenderloin with the honey sriracha mixture.
4. Place the tenderloin on the grill and roast for about 50 minutes to 1 hour, turning occasionally, until the internal temperature reaches 145°F.
5. Let the tenderloin rest for 10 minutes before slicing. Serve warm.

Asian Ginger Garlic Pork Chops

🕐 *PREP TIME: **15** MINUTES, PLUS **30** MINUTES FOR MARINATING, COOK TIME: **20** MINUTES, SERVES: **4***

🍹 **INGREDIENTS:**

- 4 pork chops
- ¼ cup soy sauce
- 2 tbsps. sesame oil
- 2 tbsps. honey
- 2 cloves garlic, minced
- 1 tbsp. grated ginger
- 1 tsp. black pepper
- Apple wood pellets

🍳 **DIRECTIONS:**

1. Preheat your Pit Boss Grill to 350°F.
2. In a small bowl, mix soy sauce, sesame oil, honey, garlic, ginger, and black pepper.
3. Marinate the pork chops in the mixture for at least 30 minutes.
4. Place the pork chops on the grill and roast for about 15-20 minutes, turning once, until the internal temperature reaches 145°F.
5. Let the pork chops rest for 5 minutes before serving. Serve warm.

Spicy Szechuan Pork Ribs

🕐 *PREP TIME: **20** MINUTES, COOK TIME: **5.5** HOURS, SERVES: **6***

🍹 **INGREDIENTS:**

- 3 racks pork ribs
- ¼ cup soy sauce
- 2 tbsps. hoisin sauce
- 2 tbsps. rice vinegar
- 1 tbsp. Szechuan peppercorns, ground
- 2 cloves garlic, minced
- 1 tsp. ginger, grated
- 1 tsp. chili flakes
- 1 tsp. black pepper
- Apple wood pellets

🍳 **DIRECTIONS:**

1. Preheat your Pit Boss Grill to 250°F.
2. In a small bowl, mix soy sauce, hoisin sauce, rice vinegar, Szechuan peppercorns, garlic, ginger, chili flakes, and black pepper.
3. Rub the ribs thoroughly with the spice mixture.
4. Place the ribs on the grill and smoke at 250°F for 3 hours.
5. Wrap the ribs in aluminum foil and continue cooking for another 2 hours.
6. Unwrap the ribs and cook for an additional 30 minutes, unwrapped, until the ribs are tender.
7. Serve warm.

Pork Tenderloin with Roasted Carrots

🕐 *PREP TIME: **15** MINUTES, COOK TIME: **30** MINUTES, SERVES: **4***

🍽 **INGREDIENTS:**
- 1 pork tenderloin (about 2 pounds)
- 6 large carrots, peeled and halved lengthwise
- ¼ cup olive oil
- 2 tbsps. fresh rosemary, chopped
- 2 tbsps. fresh thyme, chopped
- 2 cloves garlic, minced
- 1 tsp. kosher salt
- 1 tsp. black pepper
- Apple wood pellets

🍴 **DIRECTIONS:**
1. Preheat your Pit Boss Grill to 400°F.
2. In a small bowl, mix olive oil, rosemary, thyme, garlic, salt, and pepper.
3. Rub the pork tenderloin with half of the herb mixture.
4. Toss the halved carrots with the remaining herb mixture.
5. Place the pork tenderloin and carrots on the grill.
6. Roast the pork tenderloin for about 25-30 minutes, or until the internal temperature reaches 145°F.
7. Meanwhile, roast the carrots until they are tender and slightly charred, about 20-25 minutes.
8. Let the pork tenderloin rest for 10 minutes before slicing. Serve warm with the roasted carrots.

Herb-Crusted Pork Crown Roast

🕐 *PREP TIME: **30** MINUTES, COOK TIME: **2** HOURS, SERVES: **8***

🍽 **INGREDIENTS:**
- 1 pork crown roast (about 6-8 pounds)
- ¼ cup olive oil
- 2 tbsps. fresh rosemary, chopped
- 2 tbsps. fresh thyme, chopped
- 4 cloves garlic, minced
- 1 tbsp. Dijon mustard
- 1 tsp. kosher salt
- 1 tsp. black pepper
- Cherry wood pellets

🍴 **DIRECTIONS:**
1. Preheat your Pit Boss Grill to 300°F.
2. In a small bowl, mix olive oil, rosemary, thyme, garlic, Dijon mustard, salt, and pepper.
3. Rub the pork crown roast with the herb mixture.
4. Place the pork crown roast on the grill and roast for about 2 hours, or until the internal temperature reaches 145°F.
5. Let the roast rest for 10 minutes before slicing. Serve warm.

Korean Gochujang Pork Belly

🕐 *PREP TIME: **20** MINUTES, COOK TIME: **5** HOURS, SERVES: **6***

🍷 **INGREDIENTS:**
- 3 pounds pork belly
- ¼ cup gochujang (Korean chili paste)
- 2 tbsps. soy sauce
- 2 tbsps. sesame oil
- 2 tbsps. honey
- 4 cloves garlic, minced
- 1 tsp. black pepper
- 1 tsp. kosher salt
- Hickory wood pellets

🍴 **DIRECTIONS:**
1. Preheat your Pit Boss Grill to 250°F.
2. In a small bowl, mix gochujang, soy sauce, sesame oil, honey, garlic, black pepper, and salt.
3. Rub the pork belly with the gochujang mixture.
4. Place the pork belly on the grill and smoke at 250°F for about 4 hours.
5. Increase the grill temperature to 375°F and cook for an additional 1 hour, basting with the remaining glaze every 20 minutes, until the pork belly is crispy.
6. Let the pork belly rest for 10 minutes before slicing. Serve warm.

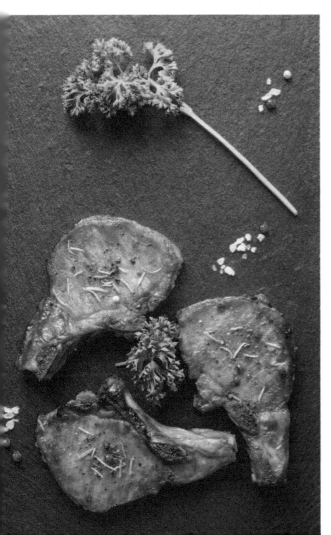

Honey Mustard Pork Cutlets

🕐 *PREP TIME: **15** MINUTES, COOK TIME: **10** MINUTES, SERVES: **4***

🍷 **INGREDIENTS:**
- 4 pork cutlets
- ¼ cup honey
- 2 tbsps. Dijon mustard
- 2 tbsps. olive oil
- 1 tsp. black pepper
- 1 tsp. kosher salt
- Maple wood pellets

🍴 **DIRECTIONS:**
1. Preheat your Pit Boss Grill to 400°F.
2. In a small bowl, mix honey, Dijon mustard, olive oil, black pepper, and salt.
3. Brush the pork cutlets with the honey mustard mixture.
4. Place the pork cutlets on the grill and grill for about 8-10 minutes, turning once, until the internal temperature reaches 145°F.
5. Let the cutlets rest for 5 minutes before serving. Serve warm.

Garlic Rosemary Pork Roast

*PREP TIME: **15** MINUTES, COOK TIME: **2** HOURS, SERVES: **6***

INGREDIENTS:
- 1 pork roast (3-4 pounds)
- 4 cloves garlic, minced
- 2 tbsps. fresh rosemary, chopped
- 2 tbsps. olive oil
- 1 tsp. kosher salt
- 1 tsp. black pepper
- Cherry wood pellets

DIRECTIONS:
1. Preheat your Pit Boss Grill to 300°F.
2. In a small bowl, mix garlic, rosemary, olive oil, salt, and pepper.
3. Rub the pork roast with the garlic rosemary mixture.
4. Place the pork roast on the grill and roast for about 2 hours, or until the internal temperature reaches 145°F.
5. Let the roast rest for 10 minutes before slicing. Serve warm.

Spiced Pork Chops with Baby Potatoes

*PREP TIME: **15** MINUTES, COOK TIME: **25** MINUTES, SERVES: **4***

INGREDIENTS:
- 4 pork chops
- 1 pound baby potatoes
- ¼ cup olive oil
- 1 tbsp. smoked paprika
- 1 tsp. cumin
- 1 tsp. garlic powder
- 1 tsp. onion powder
- 1 tsp. kosher salt
- 1 tsp. black pepper
- Mesquite wood pellets

DIRECTIONS:
1. Preheat your Pit Boss Grill to 450°F with the flame broiler open.
2. In a small bowl, mix olive oil, smoked paprika, cumin, garlic powder, onion powder, salt, and pepper.
3. Rub the pork chops with half of the spice mixture.
4. Toss the baby potatoes with the remaining spice mixture.
5. Place the pork chops and potatoes on the grill.
6. Grill the pork chops for about 15-20 minutes, turning once, until the internal temperature reaches 145°F.
7. Meanwhile, grill the potatoes until they are tender and slightly charred, about 20-25 minutes.
8. Let the pork chops rest for 5 minutes before serving. Serve warm with the grilled potatoes.

Chapter 4: Lamb

Grilled Herb Lamb Chops

🕐 *PREP TIME: **20** MINUTES, COOK TIME: **10** MINUTES, SERVES: **4***

🍷 **INGREDIENTS:**
- 8 lamb chops
- ¼ cup olive oil
- 2 tbsps. fresh rosemary, chopped
- 2 tbsps. fresh thyme, chopped
- 4 cloves garlic, minced
- 1 tsp. kosher salt
- 1 tsp. black pepper
- Mesquite wood pellets

🍳 **DIRECTIONS:**
1. Preheat your Pit Boss Grill to 450°F with the flame broiler open.
2. In a small bowl, mix olive oil, rosemary, thyme, garlic, salt, and pepper.
3. Rub the lamb chops with the herb mixture.
4. Place the lamb chops on the grill.
5. Grill the lamb chops directly over the flame for about 4-5 minutes per side, until the internal temperature reaches 145°F for medium-rare.
6. Let the lamb chops rest for 5 minutes before serving. Serve warm.

Smoky Lamb Shoulder Roast

🕐 *PREP TIME: **20** MINUTES, COOK TIME: **6** HOURS, SERVES: **6***

🍷 **INGREDIENTS:**
- 1 lamb shoulder (4-5 pounds)
- 2 tbsps. kosher salt
- 2 tbsps. black pepper
- 2 tbsps. garlic powder
- 2 tbsps. onion powder
- 1 cup chicken broth
- Hickory wood pellets

🍳 **DIRECTIONS:**
1. Preheat your Pit Boss Grill to 250°F.
2. Combine salt, pepper, garlic powder, and onion powder. Rub the lamb shoulder thoroughly with the spice mix.
3. Place the lamb shoulder on the grill.
4. Smoke at 250°F for about 4 hours.
5. Wrap the lamb shoulder in aluminum foil with the chicken broth inside and return to the grill.
6. Continue cooking for an additional 2 hours, or until the internal temperature reaches 195°F.
7. Let the lamb shoulder rest for 30 minutes before shredding. Serve warm.

Curry-Spiced Lamb Skewers

🕐 *PREP TIME: **20** MINUTES, PLUS **30** MINUTES FOR MARINATING, COOK TIME: **12** MINUTES, SERVES: **4***

🍴 **INGREDIENTS:**
- 2 pounds lamb leg, cut into cubes
- ¼ cup plain yogurt
- 2 tbsps. curry powder
- 1 tbsp. lemon juice
- 4 cloves garlic, minced
- 1 tsp. kosher salt
- 1 tsp. black pepper
- Pecan wood pellets

🍳 **DIRECTIONS:**
1. Preheat your Pit Boss Grill to 450°F with the flame broiler open.
2. In a large bowl, mix yogurt, curry powder, lemon juice, garlic, salt, and pepper.
3. Add the lamb cubes to the bowl and toss to coat evenly. Marinate for at least 30 minutes.
4. Thread the lamb onto skewers.
5. Grill the skewers directly over the flame for 10-12 minutes, turning occasionally, until the lamb is cooked to your desired doneness.
6. Serve warm.

Lemon Rosemary Lamb Rack

🕐 *PREP TIME: **20** MINUTES, COOK TIME: **45** MINUTES, SERVES: **4***

🍴 **INGREDIENTS:**
- 1 rack of lamb (8 ribs)
- ¼ cup olive oil
- 2 tbsps. fresh rosemary, chopped
- 2 tbsps. lemon zest
- 4 cloves garlic, minced
- 1 tsp. kosher salt
- 1 tsp. black pepper
- Apple wood pellets

🍳 **DIRECTIONS:**
1. Preheat your Pit Boss Grill to 450°F with the flame broiler open.
2. In a small bowl, mix olive oil, rosemary, lemon zest, garlic, salt, and pepper.
3. Rub the rack of lamb with the herb mixture.
4. Place the lamb on the grill and sear directly over the flame for 4-5 minutes per side.
5. Close the flame broiler and reduce the temperature to 300°F. Cook the lamb for an additional 30-35 minutes, or until the internal temperature reaches 145°F for medium-rare.
6. Let the lamb rest for 10 minutes before slicing. Serve warm.

Moroccan Lamb Tagine

🕐 *PREP TIME: **30** MINUTES, COOK TIME: **2** HOURS, SERVES: **6***

🍽 **INGREDIENTS:**
- 2 pounds lamb shoulder, cut into chunks
- 1 onion, chopped
- 2 cloves garlic, minced
- 1 tbsp. ground cumin
- 1 tbsp. ground coriander
- 1 tsp. ground cinnamon
- 1 tsp. ground ginger
- 1 cup chicken broth
- 1 cup diced tomatoes
- ½ cup dried apricots, chopped
- ¼ cup fresh cilantro, chopped
- 1 tbsp. olive oil
- Pecan wood pellets

🍴 **DIRECTIONS:**
1. Preheat your Pit Boss Grill to 300°F.
2. In a Dutch oven, heat olive oil and sauté the onion and garlic until soft.
3. Add the lamb chunks and brown on all sides.
4. Stir in cumin, coriander, cinnamon, and ginger, and cook for 1 minute.
5. Add chicken broth, diced tomatoes, and dried apricots. Bring to a simmer.
6. Place the Dutch oven on the grill and cook for about 2 hours, or until the lamb is tender.
7. Stir in fresh cilantro before serving. Serve warm.

Balsamic Glazed Lamb Shank

🕐 *PREP TIME: **20** MINUTES, COOK TIME: **2** HOURS, SERVES: **4***

🍽 **INGREDIENTS:**
- 4 lamb shanks
- ¼ cup balsamic vinegar
- 2 tbsps. honey
- 2 tbsps. olive oil
- 4 cloves garlic, minced
- 1 tsp. black pepper
- 1 tsp. kosher salt
- Hickory wood pellets

🍴 **DIRECTIONS:**
1. Preheat your Pit Boss Grill to 300°F.
2. In a small bowl, mix balsamic vinegar, honey, olive oil, garlic, black pepper, and salt.
3. Rub the lamb shanks with the balsamic mixture.
4. Place the lamb shanks on the grill and roast for about 2 hours, basting with the remaining mixture every 30 minutes, until the lamb is tender and the internal temperature reaches 145°F.
5. Serve warm.

Lemon Garlic Lamb Chops with Grilled Asparagus

⏱ *PREP TIME: **15** MINUTES, COOK TIME: **15** MINUTES, SERVES: **4***

🍸 **INGREDIENTS:**

- 4 lamb chops
- 1 bunch asparagus, trimmed
- ¼ cup olive oil
- 2 tbsps. lemon juice
- 4 cloves garlic, minced
- 1 tbsp. fresh parsley, chopped
- 1 tsp. kosher salt
- 1 tsp. black pepper
- Apple wood pellets

🍳 **DIRECTIONS:**

1. Preheat your Pit Boss Grill to 450°F with the flame broiler open.
2. In a small bowl, mix olive oil, lemon juice, garlic, parsley, salt, and pepper.
3. Rub the lamb chops with half of the lemon garlic mixture.
4. Toss the asparagus with the remaining lemon garlic mixture.
5. Place the lamb chops and asparagus on the grill.
6. Grill the lamb chops directly over the flame for about 4 minutes per side, until the internal temperature reaches 145°F for medium-rare.
7. Meanwhile, grill the asparagus until they are tender and slightly charred, about 10-15 minutes.
8. Let the lamb chops rest for 5 minutes before serving. Serve warm with the grilled asparagus.

Garlic Mint Lamb Steaks

⏱ *PREP TIME: **15** MINUTES, COOK TIME: **14** MINUTES, SERVES: **6***

🍸 **INGREDIENTS:**

- 6 lamb steaks
- ¼ cup olive oil
- 2 tbsps. fresh mint, chopped
- 4 cloves garlic, minced
- 1 tsp. black pepper
- 1 tsp. kosher salt
- Cherry wood pellets

🍳 **DIRECTIONS:**

1. Preheat your Pit Boss Grill to 400°F.
2. In a small bowl, mix olive oil, mint, garlic, black pepper, and salt.
3. Rub the lamb steaks with the garlic mint mixture.
4. Place the lamb steaks on the grill and grill for about 6-7 minutes per side, until the internal temperature reaches 145°F for medium-rare.
5. Let the lamb steaks rest for 5 minutes before serving. Serve warm.

Dijon Herb-Crusted Lamb Leg

🕐 PREP TIME: **20** MINUTES, COOK TIME: **1.5** HOURS, SERVES: **6**

🍷 INGREDIENTS:
- 1 leg of lamb (5-6 pounds)
- ¼ cup Dijon mustard
- 2 tbsps. fresh rosemary, chopped
- 2 tbsps. fresh thyme, chopped
- 4 cloves garlic, minced
- 1 tbsp. olive oil
- 1 tsp. kosher salt
- 1 tsp. black pepper
- Hickory wood pellets

🍴 DIRECTIONS:
1. Preheat your Pit Boss Grill to 300°F.
2. In a small bowl, mix Dijon mustard, rosemary, thyme, garlic, olive oil, salt, and pepper.
3. Rub the leg of lamb with the mustard herb mixture.
4. Place the lamb on the grill and cook for about 1.5 hours, or until the internal temperature reaches 145°F for medium-rare.
5. Let the lamb rest for 10 minutes before slicing. Serve warm.

Chili-Rubbed Lamb Loin

🕐 PREP TIME: **15** MINUTES, COOK TIME: **30** MINUTES, SERVES: **4**

🍷 INGREDIENTS:
- 2 lamb loins (about 1.5 pounds each)
- 2 tbsps. chili powder
- 1 tbsp. cumin
- 1 tbsp. paprika
- 1 tsp. garlic powder
- 1 tsp. onion powder
- 1 tsp. kosher salt
- 1 tsp. black pepper
- Mesquite wood pellets

🍴 DIRECTIONS:
1. Preheat your Pit Boss Grill to 400°F.
2. In a small bowl, mix chili powder, cumin, paprika, garlic powder, onion powder, salt, and pepper.
3. Rub the lamb loins with the chili mixture.
4. Place the lamb loins on the grill and grill for about 30 minutes, turning occasionally, until the internal temperature reaches 145°F for medium-rare.
5. Let the lamb rest for 10 minutes before slicing. Serve warm.

Garlic Herb Lamb Ribs

🕐 *PREP TIME: **20** MINUTES, COOK TIME: **2** HOURS, SERVES: **4***

🏆 **INGREDIENTS:**
- 2 racks lamb ribs
- ¼ cup olive oil
- 2 tbsps. fresh rosemary, chopped
- 2 tbsps. fresh thyme, chopped
- 4 cloves garlic, minced
- 1 tsp. black pepper
- 1 tsp. kosher salt
- Pecan wood pellets

🍳 **DIRECTIONS:**
1. Preheat your Pit Boss Grill to 300°F.
2. In a small bowl, mix olive oil, rosemary, thyme, garlic, black pepper, and salt.
3. Rub the lamb ribs with the garlic herb mixture.
4. Place the lamb ribs on the grill and cook for about 2 hours, basting with the remaining mixture every 30 minutes, until the lamb is tender.
5. Serve warm.

BBQ Lamb Brisket

🕐 *PREP TIME: **20** MINUTES, COOK TIME: **6** HOURS, SERVES: **6***

🏆 **INGREDIENTS:**
- 1 lamb brisket (4-5 pounds)
- ¼ cup BBQ sauce
- 2 tbsps. olive oil
- 2 tbsps. smoked paprika
- 2 tbsps. brown sugar
- 1 tbsp. garlic powder
- 1 tbsp. onion powder
- 1 tsp. black pepper
- 1 tsp. kosher salt
- Hickory wood pellets

🍳 **DIRECTIONS:**
1. Preheat your Pit Boss Grill to 250°F.
2. In a small bowl, mix olive oil, smoked paprika, brown sugar, garlic powder, onion powder, black pepper, and salt.
3. Rub the lamb brisket with the spice mixture.
4. Place the lamb brisket on the grill and smoke at 250°F for about 4 hours.
5. Wrap the brisket in aluminum foil, brush with BBQ sauce, and continue cooking for an additional 2 hours, or until the internal temperature reaches 195°F.
6. Let the brisket rest for 30 minutes before slicing. Serve warm with extra BBQ sauce on the side.

Citrus Marinated Lamb Chops

🕐 *PREP TIME: **20** MINUTES, COOK TIME: **10** MINUTES, SERVES: **4***

🍽 **INGREDIENTS:**
- 8 lamb chops
- ¼ cup olive oil
- 2 tbsps. lemon juice
- 2 tbsps. orange juice
- 4 cloves garlic, minced
- 1 tsp. black pepper
- 1 tsp. kosher salt
- Mesquite wood pellets

🍴 **DIRECTIONS:**
1. Preheat your Pit Boss Grill to 450°F with the flame broiler open.
2. In a small bowl, mix olive oil, lemon juice, orange juice, garlic, black pepper, and salt.
3. Rub the lamb chops with the citrus marinade.
4. Place the lamb chops on the grill.
5. Grill the lamb chops directly over the flame for about 4-5 minutes per side, until the internal temperature reaches 145°F for medium-rare.
6. Let the lamb chops rest for 5 minutes before serving. Serve warm.

Rosemary Lamb Steaks with Grilled Eggplant

🕐 *PREP TIME: **15** MINUTES, COOK TIME: **15** MINUTES, SERVES: **4***

🍽 **INGREDIENTS:**
- 4 lamb steaks
- 2 large eggplants, sliced into rounds
- ¼ cup olive oil
- 2 tbsps. fresh rosemary, chopped
- 4 cloves garlic, minced
- 1 tsp. black pepper
- 1 tsp. kosher salt
- Mesquite wood pellets

🍴 **DIRECTIONS:**
1. Preheat your Pit Boss Grill to 450°F with the flame broiler open.
2. In a small bowl, mix olive oil, rosemary, garlic, black pepper, and salt.
3. Rub the lamb steaks with half of the rosemary mixture.
4. Brush the eggplant slices with the remaining rosemary mixture.
5. Place the lamb steaks and eggplant slices on the grill.
6. Grill the lamb steaks directly over the flame for about 4-5 minutes per side, until the internal temperature reaches 145°F for medium-rare.
7. Meanwhile, grill the eggplant slices until they are tender and slightly charred, about 10-15 minutes.
8. Let the lamb steaks rest for 5 minutes before serving. Serve warm with the grilled eggplant.

Chapter 5: Vegetables

Honey Grilled Carrots and Brussels Sprouts

🕐 *PREP TIME: **15** MINUTES, COOK TIME: **20** MINUTES, SERVES: **6***

🏆 **INGREDIENTS:**
- 6 large carrots, peeled and halved lengthwise
- 1 pound Brussels sprouts, halved
- ¼ cup honey
- 4 cloves garlic, minced
- ¼ cup olive oil
- 2 tsps. black pepper
- 2 tsps. kosher salt
- Cherry wood pellets

🍳 **DIRECTIONS:**
1. Preheat your Pit Boss Grill to 400°F.
2. In a small bowl, mix honey, garlic, olive oil, black pepper, and salt.
3. Toss the carrots and Brussels sprouts in the honey garlic mixture.
4. Place the carrots and Brussels sprouts on the grill.
5. Grill the vegetables for about 10 minutes per side, until tender and slightly charred.
6. Serve warm.

Glazed Grilled Asparagus and Portobello Mushrooms

🕐 *PREP TIME: **10** MINUTES, COOK TIME: **16** MINUTES, SERVES: **4***

🏆 **INGREDIENTS:**
- 1 bunch asparagus, trimmed
- 4 large Portobello mushrooms, stems removed
- ¼ cup balsamic vinegar
- 2 tbsps. olive oil
- 4 cloves garlic, minced
- 1 tsp. kosher salt
- 1 tsp. black pepper
- Apple wood pellets

🍳 **DIRECTIONS:**
1. Preheat your Pit Boss Grill to 400°F.
2. In a small bowl, mix balsamic vinegar, olive oil, garlic, salt, and pepper.
3. Toss the asparagus and Portobello mushrooms in the balsamic mixture.
4. Place the asparagus and mushrooms on the grill.
5. Grill the asparagus for about 5 minutes per side and the mushrooms for about 7-8 minutes per side, until tender and slightly charred.
6. Serve warm.

Grilled Cauliflower Steaks

🕐 *PREP TIME: **10** MINUTES, COOK TIME: **20** MINUTES, SERVES: **4***

🍴 **INGREDIENTS:**
- 2 large cauliflower heads, sliced into 1-inch thick steaks
- ¼ cup olive oil
- 2 tsps. smoked paprika
- 2 tsps. garlic powder
- 2 tsps. onion powder
- 2 tsps. kosher salt
- 2 tsps. black pepper
- Pecan wood pellets

🍳 **DIRECTIONS:**
1. Preheat your Pit Boss Grill to 400°F.
2. In a small bowl, mix olive oil, smoked paprika, garlic powder, onion powder, salt, and pepper.
3. Brush the cauliflower steaks with the olive oil mixture.
4. Place the cauliflower steaks directly on the grill.
5. Grill for about 10 minutes per side, until tender and grill marks appear.
6. Serve warm.

Sweet Potatoes and Butternut Squash with Rosemary

🕐 *PREP TIME: **15** MINUTES, COOK TIME: **30** MINUTES, SERVES: **6***

🍴 **INGREDIENTS:**
- 3 large sweet potatoes, peeled and sliced into rounds
- 1 butternut squash, peeled and cut into chunks
- ¼ cup olive oil
- 4 cloves garlic, minced
- 2 tbsps. fresh rosemary, chopped
- 1 tsp. kosher salt
- 1 tsp. black pepper
- Cherry wood pellets

🍳 **DIRECTIONS:**
1. Preheat your Pit Boss Grill to 400°F.
2. In a small bowl, mix olive oil, garlic, rosemary, salt, and pepper.
3. Toss the sweet potatoes and butternut squash in the olive oil mixture.
4. Place the sweet potatoes and butternut squash on the grill.
5. Grill the sweet potatoes for about 10 minutes per side and the butternut squash for about 12-15 minutes per side, until tender and slightly charred.
6. Serve warm.

Grilled Broccoli and Cauliflower

🕐 *PREP TIME: **15** MINUTES, COOK TIME: **20** MINUTES, SERVES: **6***

🍸 INGREDIENTS:
- 1 large head of broccoli, cut into florets
- 1 large cauliflower, cut into florets
- ¼ cup olive oil
- 4 cloves garlic, minced
- 2 tsps. kosher salt
- 2 tsps. black pepper
- Hickory wood pellets

🍳 DIRECTIONS:
1. Preheat your Pit Boss Grill to 450°F with the flame broiler open.
2. In a small bowl, mix olive oil, garlic, salt, and pepper.
3. Toss the broccoli and cauliflower florets in the olive oil mixture.
4. Place the broccoli and cauliflower on the grill.
5. Grill the vegetables for about 10 minutes per side, until tender and slightly charred.
6. Serve warm.

Cabbage Wedges with Bacon and Blue Cheese

🕐 *PREP TIME: **15** MINUTES, COOK TIME: **20** MINUTES, SERVES: **6***

🍸 INGREDIENTS:
- 1 large head of cabbage, cut into wedges
- 6 slices bacon, cooked and crumbled
- ¼ cup olive oil
- 2 cloves garlic, minced
- 2 tbsps. blue cheese crumbles
- 2 tsps. kosher salt
- 2 tsps. black pepper
- Mesquite wood pellets

🍳 DIRECTIONS:
1. Preheat your Pit Boss Grill to high temperature with the flame broiler open.
2. In a small bowl, mix olive oil, garlic, salt, and pepper.
3. Brush the cabbage wedges with the olive oil mixture.
4. Place the cabbage wedges on the grill.
5. Grill the cabbage wedges for about 10 minutes per side, until tender and slightly charred.
6. Sprinkle with crumbled bacon and blue cheese before serving. Serve warm.

Grilled Baby Bok Choy with Soy-Ginger Glaze

🕐 *PREP TIME: **10** MINUTES, COOK TIME: **8** MINUTES, SERVES: **6***

🍸 **INGREDIENTS:**
- 6 baby bok choy, halved lengthwise
- ¼ cup soy sauce
- 2 tbsps. rice vinegar
- 1 tbsp. honey
- 1 tbsp. fresh ginger, grated
- 2 cloves garlic, minced
- 1 tsp. sesame oil
- 2 tsps. sesame seeds
- Pecan wood pellets

🍳 **DIRECTIONS:**
1. Preheat your Pit Boss Grill to 400°F.
2. In a small bowl, mix soy sauce, rice vinegar, honey, ginger, garlic, and sesame oil.
3. Brush the bok choy halves with the soy-ginger mixture.
4. Place the bok choy directly on the grill.
5. Grill for about 4 minutes per side, until tender and slightly charred.
6. Sprinkle with sesame seeds before serving.
7. Serve warm.

Stuffed Bell Peppers with Quinoa and Black Beans

🕐 *PREP TIME: **20** MINUTES, COOK TIME: **30** MINUTES, SERVES: **6***

🍸 **INGREDIENTS:**
- 6 bell peppers, halved and seeded
- 2 cups cooked quinoa
- 1 can black beans, drained and rinsed
- 1 cup corn kernels
- ¼ cup olive oil
- 4 cloves garlic, minced
- 1 tsp. cumin
- 1 tsp. smoked paprika
- 2 tsps. kosher salt
- 2 tsps. black pepper
- Pecan wood pellets

🍳 **DIRECTIONS:**
1. Preheat your Pit Boss Grill to 400°F.
2. In a large bowl, mix cooked quinoa, black beans, corn, olive oil, garlic, cumin, smoked paprika, salt, and pepper.
3. Stuff the bell pepper halves with the quinoa mixture.
4. Place the stuffed bell peppers on the grill.
5. Cook the bell peppers for about 30 minutes, until the peppers are tender and slightly charred.
6. Serve warm.

Grilled Red Onion Rings

🕐 *PREP TIME: **10** MINUTES, COOK TIME: **16** MINUTES, SERVES: **8***

🍸 **INGREDIENTS:**
- 4 large red onions, sliced into thick rings
- ¼ cup olive oil
- 4 cloves garlic, minced
- 2 tsps. balsamic vinegar
- 2 tsps. kosher salt
- 2 tsps. black pepper
- Mesquite wood pellets

🍴 **DIRECTIONS:**
1. Preheat your Pit Boss Grill to 450°F with the flame broiler open.
2. In a small bowl, mix olive oil, garlic, balsamic vinegar, salt, and pepper.
3. Brush the red onion rings with the mixture.
4. Place the onion rings on the grill.
5. Grill the onion rings directly over the flame for about 7-8 minutes per side, until tender and slightly charred.
6. Serve warm.

Grilled Sweet Potatoes and Peppers with Thyme

🕐 *PREP TIME: **15** MINUTES, COOK TIME: **20** MINUTES, SERVES: **6***

🍸 **INGREDIENTS:**
- 3 large sweet potatoes, sliced into rounds
- 3 bell peppers, halved and seeded
- ¼ cup olive oil
- 4 cloves garlic, minced
- 2 tbsps. fresh thyme, chopped
- 2 tsps. kosher salt
- 2 tsps. black pepper
- Apple wood pellets

🍴 **DIRECTIONS:**
1. Preheat your Pit Boss Grill to 450°F with the flame broiler open.
2. In a small bowl, mix olive oil, garlic, thyme, salt, and pepper.
3. Toss the sweet potatoes and bell peppers in the olive oil mixture.
4. Place the sweet potatoes and bell peppers on the grill.
5. Grill the sweet potatoes for about 10 minutes per side and the bell peppers for about 7-8 minutes per side, until tender and slightly charred.
6. Serve warm.

Grilled Corn on the Cob with Chili Lime Butter

🕐 *PREP TIME: **10** MINUTES, COOK TIME: **16** MINUTES, SERVES: **6***

🍸 INGREDIENTS:
- 6 ears of corn, husked
- ¼ cup butter, melted
- 2 tbsps. lime juice
- 1 tbsp. chili powder
- 1 tsp. garlic powder
- 2 tsps. kosher salt
- 2 tsps. black pepper
- Mesquite wood pellets

🍳 DIRECTIONS:
1. Preheat your Pit Boss Grill to 450°F with the flame broiler open.
2. In a small bowl, mix melted butter, lime juice, chili powder, garlic powder, salt, and pepper.
3. Brush the corn with the chili lime butter mixture.
4. Place the corn on the grill.
5. Grill the corn directly over the flame for about 7-8 minutes per side, until the kernels are tender and slightly charred.
6. Serve warm.

Eggplant and Tomato Stacks with Basil

🕐 *PREP TIME: **15** MINUTES, COOK TIME: **16** MINUTES, SERVES: **6***

🍸 INGREDIENTS:
- 2 large eggplants, sliced into rounds
- 6 large tomatoes, sliced into rounds
- ¼ cup olive oil
- 4 cloves garlic, minced
- 2 tbsps. fresh basil, chopped
- 2 tsps. kosher salt
- 2 tsps. black pepper
- Mesquite wood pellets

🍳 DIRECTIONS:
1. Preheat your Pit Boss Grill to 400°F.
2. In a small bowl, mix olive oil, garlic, basil, salt, and pepper.
3. Brush the eggplant and tomato slices with the olive oil mixture.
4. Place the eggplant slices on the grill.
5. Grill the eggplant for about 7-8 minutes per side, until tender and slightly charred.
6. Meanwhile, add the tomato slices to the grill and cook for about 3-4 minutes per side, until tender.
7. Stack the grilled eggplant and tomato slices, alternating with a sprinkle of basil between layers.
8. Serve warm.

Grilled Zucchini and Summer Squash

🕐 *PREP TIME: **10** MINUTES, COOK TIME: **14** MINUTES, SERVES: **6***

🍸 **INGREDIENTS:**
- 3 large zucchinis, sliced into rounds
- 3 large summer squashes, sliced into rounds
- ¼ cup olive oil
- 4 cloves garlic, minced
- 2 tsps. kosher salt
- 2 tsps. black pepper
- ½ cup grated Parmesan cheese
- Cherry wood pellets

🍲 **DIRECTIONS:**
1. Preheat your Pit Boss Grill to 450°F with the flame broiler open.
2. In a small bowl, mix olive oil, garlic, salt, and pepper.
3. Toss the zucchini and summer squash slices in the olive oil mixture.
4. Place the zucchini and summer squash slices on the grill.
5. Grill the vegetables for about 5-7 minutes per side, until tender and slightly charred.
6. Sprinkle with grated Parmesan cheese before serving. Serve warm.

Lemon Herb Grilled Artichokes

🕐 *PREP TIME: **15** MINUTES, COOK TIME: **20** MINUTES, SERVES: **6***

🍸 **INGREDIENTS:**
- 6 large artichokes, halved and cleaned
- ¼ cup olive oil
- 4 cloves garlic, minced
- 4 tbsps. lemon juice
- 2 tbsps. fresh parsley, chopped
- 2 tsps. kosher salt
- 2 tsps. black pepper
- Mesquite wood pellets

🍲 **DIRECTIONS:**
1. Preheat your Pit Boss Grill to 400°F.
2. In a small bowl, mix olive oil, garlic, lemon juice, parsley, salt, and pepper.
3. Brush the artichokes with the lemon herb mixture.
4. Place the artichokes on the grill.
5. Grill the artichokes for about 10 minutes per side, until tender and slightly charred.
6. Serve warm.

Chapter 6: Fish and Seafood

Spicy Cajun Grilled Catfish

🕐 *PREP TIME: **15** MINUTES, COOK TIME: **10** MINUTES, SERVES: **6***

🍸 **INGREDIENTS:**
- 6 catfish fillets
- ⅓ cup olive oil
- 3 tbsps. Cajun seasoning
- 1½ tbsps. paprika
- 2 tsps. garlic powder
- 2 tsps. onion powder
- 2 tsps. black pepper
- 2 tsps. kosher salt
- Mesquite wood pellets

😋 **DIRECTIONS:**
1. Preheat your Pit Boss Grill to 450°F with the flame broiler open.
2. In a small bowl, mix olive oil, Cajun seasoning, paprika, garlic powder, onion powder, black pepper, and salt.
3. Rub the catfish fillets with the spice mixture.
4. Place the catfish fillets on the grill.
5. Sear the catfish directly over the flame for about 5 minutes per side, until the internal temperature reaches 145°F and the fish is opaque and flakes easily.
6. Serve warm.

Garlic Butter Lobster Tails

🕐 *PREP TIME: **20** MINUTES, COOK TIME: **5** MINUTES, SERVES: **6***

🍸 **INGREDIENTS:**
- 6 lobster tails
- ⅓ cup melted butter
- 6 cloves garlic, minced
- 2 tbsps. fresh parsley, chopped
- 2 tbsps. lemon juice
- 2 tsps. paprika
- 2 tsps. kosher salt
- 2 tsps. black pepper
- Pecan wood pellets

😋 **DIRECTIONS:**
1. Preheat your Pit Boss Grill to 450°F with the flame broiler open.
2. In a small bowl, mix melted butter, garlic, parsley, lemon juice, paprika, salt, and pepper.
3. Brush the lobster tails with the garlic butter mixture.
4. Place the lobster tails on the grill, shell side down.
5. Grill the lobster tails directly over the flame for about 5 minutes, until the meat is opaque and cooked through.
6. Serve warm.

Teriyaki Grilled Tuna Steaks

🕐 PREP TIME: **15** MINUTES, PLUS **15** MINUTES FOR MARINATING, COOK TIME: **6** MINUTES, SERVES: **6**

🍸 INGREDIENTS:
- 6 tuna steaks
- ½ cup soy sauce
- 4 tbsps. honey
- 4 tbsps. rice vinegar
- 6 cloves garlic, minced
- 3 tbsps. grated ginger
- 2 tsps. black pepper
- 2 tsps. sesame oil
- Mesquite wood pellets

🍲 DIRECTIONS:
1. Preheat your Pit Boss Grill to 450°F with the flame broiler open.
2. In a small bowl, mix soy sauce, honey, rice vinegar, garlic, ginger, black pepper, and sesame oil.
3. Marinate the tuna steaks in the mixture for at least 15 minutes.
4. Place the tuna steaks on the grill.
5. Grill the tuna steaks directly over the flame for about 3 minutes per side for medium-rare, or longer to your desired doneness.
6. Serve warm.

Honey Lime Grilled Scallops

🕐 PREP TIME: **20** MINUTES, COOK TIME: **6** MINUTES, SERVES: **6**

🍸 INGREDIENTS:
- 3 pounds large scallops
- ½ cup honey
- 4 tbsps. lime juice
- 4 tbsps. olive oil
- 4 cloves garlic, minced
- 2 tsps. black pepper
- 2 tsps. kosher salt
- Cherry wood pellets

🍲 DIRECTIONS:
1. Preheat your Pit Boss Grill to 450°F with the flame broiler open.
2. In a small bowl, mix honey, lime juice, olive oil, garlic, black pepper, and salt.
3. Toss the scallops in the mixture to coat.
4. Place the scallops on skewers for easier grilling.
5. Grill the scallops directly over the flame for about 3 minutes per side, until they are opaque and cooked through.
6. Serve warm.

Cedar Plank Grilled Trout

🕐 *PREP TIME: 30 MINUTES, COOK TIME: 12 MINUTES, SERVES: 8*

🍸 **INGREDIENTS:**
- 4 trout fillets
- ½ cup olive oil
- 4 tbsps. fresh rosemary, chopped
- 4 tbsps. fresh thyme, chopped
- 8 cloves garlic, minced
- 2 lemons, sliced
- 2 tsps. kosher salt
- 2 tsps. black pepper
- Cedar wood planks, soaked in water for at least 1 hour
- Cherry wood pellets

🍳 **DIRECTIONS:**
1. Preheat your Pit Boss Grill to 400°F.
2. In a small bowl, mix olive oil, rosemary, thyme, garlic, salt, and pepper.
3. Rub the trout fillets with the herb mixture.
4. Place the trout fillets on the soaked cedar planks and top with lemon slices.
5. Place the cedar planks on the grill.
6. Grill the trout for about 10-12 minutes, or until the internal temperature reaches 145°F and the fish is opaque and flakes easily.
7. Serve warm.

Smoky Chipotle Grilled Shrimp

🕐 *PREP TIME: 20 MINUTES, COOK TIME: 6 MINUTES, SERVES: 8*

🍸 **INGREDIENTS:**
- 4 pounds large shrimp, peeled and deveined
- ½ cup olive oil
- 4 tbsps. chipotle chili powder
- 4 cloves garlic, minced
- 2 tbsps. lime juice
- 2 tsps. kosher salt
- 2 tsps. black pepper
- Pecan wood pellets

🍳 **DIRECTIONS:**
1. Preheat your Pit Boss Grill to 450°F with the flame broiler open.
2. In a large bowl, mix olive oil, chipotle chili powder, garlic, lime juice, salt, and pepper.
3. Toss the shrimp in the mixture to coat.
4. Thread the shrimp onto skewers for easier grilling.
5. Grill the shrimp skewers directly over the flame for about 3 minutes per side, until they are opaque and cooked through.
6. Serve warm.

Caribbean Jerk Grilled Snapper

⏱ *PREP TIME: **20** MINUTES, COOK TIME: **20** MINUTES, SERVES: **4***

🍸 **INGREDIENTS:**
- 4 whole snappers, cleaned and scaled
- ½ cup olive oil
- 4 tbsps. jerk seasoning
- 4 cloves garlic, minced
- 4 tbsps. lime juice
- 2 tsps. kosher salt
- 2 tsps. black pepper
- Mesquite wood pellets

🍴 **DIRECTIONS:**
1. Preheat your Pit Boss Grill to 450°F with the flame broiler open.
2. In a small bowl, mix olive oil, jerk seasoning, garlic, lime juice, salt, and pepper.
3. Rub the snappers with the jerk mixture, inside and out.
4. Place the snappers on the grill.
5. Grill the snappers directly over the flame for about 10 minutes per side, until the internal temperature reaches 145°F and the fish is opaque and flakes easily.
6. Serve warm.

Grilled Mahi Mahi with Mango Salsa

⏱ *PREP TIME: **15** MINUTES, COOK TIME: **16** MINUTES, SERVES: **4***

🍸 **INGREDIENTS:**
- 4 mahi mahi fillets
- ¼ cup olive oil
- 2 tbsps. lime juice
- 1 tbsp. chili powder
- 1 tsp. garlic powder
- 1 tsp. kosher salt
- 1 tsp. black pepper
- For the Mango Salsa:
- 2 ripe mangoes, diced
- ½ red onion, finely chopped
- ½ cup fresh cilantro, chopped
- 2 tbsps. lime juice
- 1 jalapeño, seeded and finely chopped (optional)
- Cherry wood pellets

🍴 **DIRECTIONS:**
1. Preheat your Pit Boss Grill to 400°F.
2. In a small bowl, mix olive oil, lime juice, chili powder, garlic powder, salt, and pepper.
3. Rub the mahi mahi fillets with the mixture.
4. Place the mahi mahi fillets on the grill.
5. Grill the mahi mahi for about 8 minutes per side, until the internal temperature reaches 145°F and the fish is opaque and flakes easily.
6. In another bowl, mix all the salsa ingredients.
7. Serve the grilled mahi mahi with mango salsa on top.

Herb-Crusted Grilled Halibut

🕐 PREP TIME: *15* MINUTES, COOK TIME: *16* MINUTES, SERVES: *8*

🍷 **INGREDIENTS:**
- 8 halibut fillets
- ½ cup olive oil
- 4 tbsps. fresh parsley, chopped
- 4 tbsps. fresh thyme, chopped
- 8 cloves garlic, minced
- 2 tsps. kosher salt
- 2 tsps. black pepper
- Cherry wood pellets

😋 **DIRECTIONS:**
1. Preheat your Pit Boss Grill to 400°F.
2. In a small bowl, mix olive oil, parsley, thyme, garlic, salt, and pepper.
3. Rub the halibut fillets with the herb mixture.
4. Place the halibut fillets on the grill.
5. Grill the halibut for about 8 minutes per side, until the internal temperature reaches 145°F and the fish is opaque and flakes easily.
6. Serve warm.

Grilled Clams with Garlic Butter

🕐 PREP TIME: *20* MINUTES, COOK TIME: *7* MINUTES, SERVES: *8*

🍷 **INGREDIENTS:**
- 4 pounds clams, scrubbed clean
- ½ cup melted butter
- 8 cloves garlic, minced
- 4 tbsps. fresh parsley, chopped
- 4 tbsps. lemon juice
- 2 tsps. black pepper
- 2 tsps. kosher salt
- Apple wood pellets

😋 **DIRECTIONS:**
1. Preheat your Pit Boss Grill to 450°F with the flame broiler open.
2. In a small bowl, mix melted butter, garlic, parsley, lemon juice, black pepper, and salt.
3. Place the clams in a single layer on the grill.
4. Grill the clams directly over the flame for about 5-7 minutes, until they open.
5. Drizzle the garlic butter mixture over the clams before serving.
6. Serve warm.

Lemon Dill Grilled Cod

🕐 *PREP TIME: **15** MINUTES, COOK TIME: **16** MINUTES, SERVES: **6***

🍸 **INGREDIENTS:**
- 6 cod fillets
- ½ cup olive oil
- 4 tbsps. lemon juice
- 4 tbsps. fresh dill, chopped
- 6 cloves garlic, minced
- 2 tsps. kosher salt
- 2 tsps. black pepper
- Cherry wood pellets

🍴 **DIRECTIONS:**
1. Preheat your Pit Boss Grill to 400°F.
2. In a small bowl, mix olive oil, lemon juice, dill, garlic, salt, and pepper.
3. Rub the cod fillets with the lemon dill mixture.
4. Place the cod fillets on the grill.
5. Grill the cod for about 8 minutes per side, until the internal temperature reaches 145°F and the fish is opaque and flakes easily.
6. Serve warm.

Grilled Whole Sea Bass with Lemon and Herbs

🕐 *PREP TIME: **20** MINUTES, COOK TIME: **30** MINUTES, SERVES: **6***

🍸 **INGREDIENTS:**
- 2 whole sea bass, cleaned and scaled
- ½ cup olive oil
- 4 cloves garlic, minced
- 4 tbsps. fresh parsley, chopped
- 4 tbsps. fresh thyme, chopped
- 2 lemons, sliced
- 2 tsps. kosher salt
- 2 tsps. black pepper
- Apple wood pellets

🍴 **DIRECTIONS:**
1. Preheat your Pit Boss Grill to 450°F with the flame broiler open.
2. In a small bowl, mix olive oil, garlic, parsley, thyme, salt, and pepper.
3. Rub the sea bass inside and out with the herb mixture.
4. Place lemon slices inside the cavity of each fish.
5. Place the sea bass on the grill.
6. Grill the sea bass directly over the flame for about 12-15 minutes per side, until the internal temperature reaches 145°F and the fish is opaque and flakes easily.
7. Serve warm.

Herb-Grilled Salmon with Asparagus

🕐 *PREP TIME: **15** MINUTES, COOK TIME: **12** MINUTES, SERVES: **4***

🍸 INGREDIENTS:
- 4 salmon fillets
- 1 bunch asparagus, trimmed
- ¼ cup olive oil
- 2 tbsps. fresh parsley, chopped
- 2 tbsps. fresh thyme, chopped
- 4 cloves garlic, minced
- 1 lemon, sliced
- 1 tsp. kosher salt
- 1 tsp. black pepper
- Cherry wood pellets

🍽 DIRECTIONS:
1. Preheat your Pit Boss Grill to 450°F with the flame broiler open.
2. In a small bowl, mix olive oil, parsley, thyme, garlic, salt, and pepper.
3. Rub the salmon fillets with the herb mixture.
4. Toss the asparagus with the remaining herb mixture.
5. Place the salmon fillets and asparagus on the grill.
6. Grill the salmon directly over the flame for about 5-6 minutes per side, until the internal temperature reaches 145°F.
7. Meanwhile, grill the asparagus for about 4-5 minutes, turning occasionally, until tender and slightly charred.
8. Serve warm with lemon slices on the side.

Sweet Chili Grilled Calamari

🕐 *PREP TIME: **20** MINUTES, COOK TIME: **6** MINUTES, SERVES: **8***

🍸 INGREDIENTS:
- 4 pounds calamari, cleaned
- ½ cup sweet chili sauce
- 4 tbsps. olive oil
- 4 cloves garlic, minced
- 4 tbsps. lime juice
- 2 tsps. kosher salt
- 2 tsps. black pepper
- Pecan wood pellets

🍽 DIRECTIONS:
1. Preheat your Pit Boss Grill to 450°F with the flame broiler open.
2. In a small bowl, mix sweet chili sauce, olive oil, garlic, lime juice, salt, and pepper.
3. Toss the calamari in the mixture to coat.
4. Place the calamari on the grill.
5. Grill the calamari directly over the flame for about 3 minutes per side, until cooked through.
6. Serve warm.

Chapter 7: Poultry

Teriyaki Grilled Chicken Thighs

🕐 *PREP TIME: **15** MINUTES, PLUS **20** MINUTES FOR MARINATING, COOK TIME: **30** MINUTES, SERVES: **6***

🍸 **INGREDIENTS:**
- 6 chicken thighs
- ½ cup soy sauce
- ¼ cup honey
- 4 cloves garlic, minced
- 2 tbsps. rice vinegar
- 2 tbsps. olive oil
- 2 tsps. grated ginger
- 2 tsps. black pepper
- 2 tsps. kosher salt
- Mesquite wood pellets

🍽 **DIRECTIONS:**
1. Preheat your Pit Boss Grill to 450°F with the flame broiler open.
2. In a small bowl, mix soy sauce, honey, garlic, rice vinegar, olive oil, ginger, black pepper, and salt.
3. Marinate the chicken thighs in the mixture for at least 20 minutes.
4. Place the chicken thighs on the grill.
5. Grill the chicken thighs directly over the flame for about 12-15 minutes per side, until the internal temperature reaches 165°F.
6. Serve warm.

Smoky Grilled Duck Breast

🕐 *PREP TIME: **15** MINUTES, PLUS **30** MINUTES FOR MARINATING, COOK TIME: **30** MINUTES, SERVES: **6***

🍸 **INGREDIENTS:**
- 6 duck breasts
- ½ cup soy sauce
- ¼ cup honey
- 4 cloves garlic, minced
- 2 tbsps. olive oil
- 2 tbsps. rice vinegar
- 2 tsps. black pepper
- 2 tsps. kosher salt
- Pecan wood pellets

🍽 **DIRECTIONS:**
1. Preheat your Pit Boss Grill to 450°F with the flame broiler open.
2. In a small bowl, mix soy sauce, honey, garlic, olive oil, rice vinegar, black pepper, and salt.
3. Marinate the duck breasts in the mixture for at least 30 minutes.
4. Place the duck breasts on the grill.
5. Grill the duck breasts directly over the flame for about 12-15 minutes per side, until the internal temperature reaches 165°F.
6. Serve warm.

Lemon Rosemary Grilled Cornish Hens

🕐 PREP TIME: **20** MINUTES, COOK TIME: **50** MINUTES, SERVES: **6**

🍷 **INGREDIENTS:**
- 6 Cornish hens
- ½ cup olive oil
- 6 cloves garlic, minced
- 4 tbsps. fresh rosemary, chopped
- 4 tbsps. lemon juice
- 2 lemons, sliced
- 2 tsps. kosher salt
- 2 tsps. black pepper
- Apple wood pellets

🍴 **DIRECTIONS:**
1. Preheat your Pit Boss Grill to 400°F.
2. In a small bowl, mix olive oil, garlic, rosemary, lemon juice, salt, and pepper.
3. Rub the Cornish hens with the mixture.
4. Place lemon slices inside the cavity of each hen.
5. Place the hens on the grill.
6. Grill the hens for about 20-25 minutes per side, until the internal temperature reaches 165°F.
7. Serve warm.

Grilled Chicken with Vegetables

🕐 PREP TIME: **20** MINUTES, COOK TIME: **30** MINUTES, SERVES: **6**

🍷 **INGREDIENTS:**
- 3 pounds chicken thighs
- 2 red bell peppers, cut into chunks
- 2 carrots, sliced into rounds
- 2 red onions, cut into chunks
- ½ cup olive oil
- 4 cloves garlic, minced
- 2 tbsps. fresh rosemary, chopped
- 2 tbsps. fresh thyme, chopped
- 2 tsps. kosher salt
- 2 tsps. black pepper
- Cherry wood pellets

🍴 **DIRECTIONS:**
1. Preheat your Pit Boss Grill to 450°F with the flame broiler open.
2. In a large bowl, mix olive oil, garlic, rosemary, thyme, salt, and pepper.
3. Toss the chicken thighs and vegetables in the mixture to coat.
4. Place the chicken thighs and vegetables on the grill.
5. Grill the chicken thighs directly over the flame for about 12-15 minutes per side, until the internal temperature reaches 165°F. Grill the vegetables for about 10-15 minutes, turning occasionally, until tender and slightly charred.
6. Serve warm.

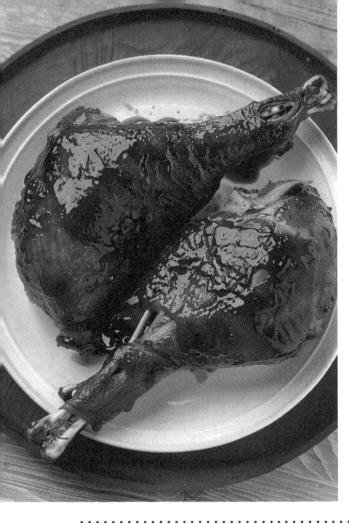

BBQ Glazed Roasted Turkey Legs

⏱ *PREP TIME: **15** MINUTES, COOK TIME: **1** HOUR, SERVES: **6***

🍸 **INGREDIENTS:**
- 6 turkey legs
- ½ cup BBQ sauce
- 4 tbsps. olive oil
- 4 cloves garlic, minced
- 2 tbsps. smoked paprika
- 2 tsps. kosher salt
- 2 tsps. black pepper
- Hickory wood pellets

🍴 **DIRECTIONS:**
1. Preheat your Pit Boss Grill to 300°F.
2. In a large bowl, mix BBQ sauce, olive oil, garlic, smoked paprika, salt, and pepper.
3. Rub the turkey legs with the mixture.
4. Place the turkey legs on the grill.
5. Roasted the turkey legs for about 30 minutes per side, until the internal temperature reaches 165°F.
6. Serve warm.

Roasted Pesto Chicken Breasts

⏱ *PREP TIME: **15** MINUTES, COOK TIME: **20** MINUTES, SERVES: **8***

🍸 **INGREDIENTS:**
- 8 chicken breasts
- ½ cup basil pesto
- 4 tbsps. olive oil
- 4 cloves garlic, minced
- 2 tsps. kosher salt
- 2 tsps. black pepper
- Cherry wood pellets

🍴 **DIRECTIONS:**
1. Preheat your Pit Boss Grill to 350°F.
2. In a small bowl, mix basil pesto, olive oil, garlic, salt, and pepper.
3. Rub the chicken breasts with the pesto mixture.
4. Place the chicken breasts on the grill.
5. Roasted the chicken breasts for about 10 minutes per side, until the internal temperature reaches 165°F.
6. Serve warm.

Grilled Chicken Caesar Salad

🕐 *PREP TIME: **20** MINUTES, COOK TIME: **20** MINUTES, SERVES: **8***

🍸 **INGREDIENTS:**
- 8 chicken breasts
- ½ cup olive oil
- 4 cloves garlic, minced
- 4 tbsps. lemon juice
- 2 tsps. kosher salt
- 2 tsps. black pepper
- Romaine lettuce, chopped
- 1 cup Caesar dressing
- 1 cup grated Parmesan cheese
- 1 cup croutons
- Apple wood pellets

🍳 **DIRECTIONS:**
1. Preheat your Pit Boss Grill to 400°F.
2. In a small bowl, mix olive oil, garlic, lemon juice, salt, and pepper.
3. Rub the chicken breasts with the mixture.
4. Place the chicken breasts on the grill.
5. Grill the chicken breasts for about 10 minutes per side, until the internal temperature reaches 165°F.
6. Let the chicken rest for 5 minutes, then slice.
7. Assemble the salad by combining chopped Romaine lettuce, Caesar dressing, Parmesan cheese, and croutons. Top with sliced grilled chicken.
8. Serve warm.

Balsamic Glazed Chicken Breasts with Portobello Mushrooms

🕐 *PREP TIME: **15** MINUTES, COOK TIME: **20** MINUTES, SERVES: **6***

🍸 **INGREDIENTS:**
- 6 chicken breasts
- 6 large Portobello mushrooms, stems removed
- ½ cup balsamic vinegar
- 4 tbsps. olive oil
- 4 cloves garlic, minced
- 2 tbsps. fresh rosemary, chopped
- 2 tbsps. fresh thyme, chopped
- 2 tsps. kosher salt
- 2 tsps. black pepper
- Hickory wood pellets

🍳 **DIRECTIONS:**
1. Preheat your Pit Boss Grill to 400°F.
2. In a small bowl, mix balsamic vinegar, olive oil, garlic, rosemary, thyme, salt, and pepper.
3. Rub the chicken breasts with half of the balsamic mixture.
4. Brush the Portobello mushrooms with the remaining balsamic mixture.
5. Place the chicken breasts and Portobello mushrooms on the grill.
6. Grill the chicken breasts for about 10 minutes per side, until the internal temperature reaches 165°F.
7. Meanwhile, grill the mushrooms for about 8-10 minutes, turning occasionally, until tender and slightly charred.
8. Serve warm.

Jerk-Spiced Grilled Chicken Wings

🕐 *PREP TIME: **15** MINUTES, COOK TIME: **30** MINUTES, SERVES: **8***

🍸 INGREDIENTS:
- 4 pounds chicken wings
- ½ cup olive oil
- 4 tbsps. jerk seasoning
- 4 cloves garlic, minced
- 2 tbsps. lime juice
- 2 tsps. kosher salt
- 2 tsps. black pepper
- Mesquite wood pellets

🍲 DIRECTIONS:
1. Preheat your Pit Boss Grill to 450°F with the flame broiler open.
2. In a large bowl, mix olive oil, jerk seasoning, garlic, lime juice, salt, and pepper.
3. Toss the chicken wings in the mixture to coat.
4. Place the chicken wings on the grill.
5. Grill the wings directly over the flame for about 15 minutes per side, until the internal temperature reaches 165°F and the skin is crispy.
6. Serve warm.

Smoky Maple Grilled Quail

🕐 *PREP TIME: **15** MINUTES, COOK TIME: **20** MINUTES, SERVES: **4***

🍸 INGREDIENTS:
- 8 quails
- ½ cup maple syrup
- 4 tbsps. soy sauce
- 4 cloves garlic, minced
- 2 tbsps. olive oil
- 2 tsps. black pepper
- 2 tsps. kosher salt
- Cherry wood pellets

🍲 DIRECTIONS:
1. Preheat your Pit Boss Grill to 400°F.
2. In a small bowl, mix maple syrup, soy sauce, garlic, olive oil, black pepper, and salt.
3. Rub the quails with the mixture.
4. Place the quails on the grill.
5. Grill the quails for about 10 minutes per side, until the internal temperature reaches 165°F.
6. Serve warm.

Roasted Whole Chicken with Herbs

🕐 *PREP TIME: **20** MINUTES, COOK TIME: **1.5** HOURS, SERVES: **6-8***

🏆 **INGREDIENTS:**
- 1 whole chicken (4-5 pounds)
- ¼ cup olive oil
- 4 cloves garlic, minced
- 2 tbsps. fresh rosemary, chopped
- 2 tbsps. fresh thyme, chopped
- 2 tbsps. fresh parsley, chopped
- 1 lemon, quartered
- 1 onion, quartered
- 2 tsps. kosher salt
- 2 tsps. black pepper
- Apple wood pellets

🍳 **DIRECTIONS:**
1. Preheat your Pit Boss Grill to 350°F.
2. In a small bowl, mix olive oil, garlic, rosemary, thyme, parsley, salt, and pepper.
3. Rinse the chicken inside and out, then pat dry with paper towels.
4. Rub the herb mixture all over the chicken, including under the skin and inside the cavity.
5. Stuff the cavity with lemon quarters and onion quarters.
6. Tie the legs together with kitchen twine and tuck the wings under the body.
7. Place the chicken directly on the grill grate, breast side up.
8. Close the grill lid and roast for about 1.5 hours, or until the internal temperature reaches 165°F and the juices run clear when the thickest part of the thigh is pierced.
9. Rotate the chicken occasionally for even cooking.
10. Let the chicken rest for 10-15 minutes before carving. Serve warm.

Thai Grilled Chicken Satay

🕐 *PREP TIME: **20** MINUTES, PLUS **30** MINUTES FOR MARINATING, COOK TIME: **10** MINUTES, SERVES: **8***

🏆 **INGREDIENTS:**
- 4 pounds chicken breasts, cut into strips
- ½ cup coconut milk
- 4 tbsps. soy sauce
- 4 tbsps. peanut butter
- 4 cloves garlic, minced
- 2 tbsps. fresh ginger, grated
- 2 tbsps. lime juice
- 2 tsps. ground coriander
- 2 tsps. turmeric powder
- 2 tsps. black pepper
- 2 tsps. kosher salt
- Pecan wood pellets

🍳 **DIRECTIONS:**
1. Preheat your Pit Boss Grill to 400°F.
2. In a large bowl, mix coconut milk, soy sauce, peanut butter, garlic, ginger, lime juice, coriander, turmeric, black pepper, and salt.
3. Marinate the chicken strips in the mixture for at least 30 minutes.
4. Thread the chicken onto skewers.
5. Grill the skewers for about 5 minutes per side, until the internal temperature of the chicken reaches 165°F.
6. Serve warm with peanut dipping sauce.

Lemon Chicken Thighs with Green Beans and Red Potatoes

🕐 *PREP TIME: **15** MINUTES, COOK TIME: **30** MINUTES, SERVES: **6***

🍸 **INGREDIENTS:**

- 6 chicken thighs
- 1 pound green beans, trimmed
- 1 pound small red potatoes, halved
- ½ cup olive oil
- 4 tbsps. lemon juice
- 4 cloves garlic, minced
- 2 tbsps. fresh parsley, chopped
- 2 tbsps. fresh thyme, chopped
- 2 tsps. kosher salt
- 2 tsps. black pepper
- Apple wood pellets

🍳 **DIRECTIONS:**

1. Preheat your Pit Boss Grill to 400°F.
2. In a small bowl, mix olive oil, lemon juice, garlic, parsley, thyme, salt, and pepper.
3. Rub the chicken thighs with the mixture.
4. Toss the green beans and red potatoes in the remaining mixture.
5. Place the chicken thighs on the grill.
6. Grill the chicken thighs for about 12-15 minutes per side, until the internal temperature reaches 165°F. Meanwhile, grill the green beans and red potatoes for about 15-20 minutes, turning occasionally, until tender and slightly charred.
7. Serve warm.

Spicy Smoked Turkey Breast

🕐 *PREP TIME: **20** MINUTES, COOK TIME: **2** HOURS, SERVES: **8***

🍸 **INGREDIENTS:**

- 1 whole turkey breast (about 4 pounds)
- ¼ cup olive oil
- 4 tbsps. chili powder
- 4 cloves garlic, minced
- 2 tbsps. smoked paprika
- 2 tbsps. brown sugar
- 2 tsps. kosher salt
- 2 tsps. black pepper
- Hickory wood pellets

🍳 **DIRECTIONS:**

1. Preheat your Pit Boss Grill to 225°F.
2. In a small bowl, mix olive oil, chili powder, garlic, smoked paprika, brown sugar, salt, and pepper.
3. Rub the turkey breast with the spice mixture.
4. Place the turkey breast on the grill.
5. Smoke the turkey breast for about 2 hours, or until the internal temperature reaches 165°F.
6. Let the turkey breast rest for 10 minutes before slicing. Serve warm.

Chapter 8: Appetizer and Snacks

Spicy Cajun Grilled Corn on the Cob

🕐 *PREP TIME: **10** MINUTES, COOK TIME: **16** MINUTES, SERVES: **8***

🍸 **INGREDIENTS:**
- 8 ears of corn, husked
- ¼ cup butter, melted
- 2 tbsps. Cajun seasoning
- 2 cloves garlic, minced
- 1 tsp. smoked paprika
- 1 tsp. black pepper
- Mesquite wood pellets

🍴 **DIRECTIONS:**
1. Preheat your Pit Boss Grill to 450°F with the flame broiler open.
2. In a small bowl, mix melted butter, Cajun seasoning, garlic, smoked paprika, and black pepper.
3. Brush the corn with the Cajun butter mixture.
4. Place the corn on the grill.
5. Grill the corn directly over the flame for about 7-8 minutes per side, until the kernels are tender and slightly charred.
6. Serve warm.

Zucchini Rolls with Goat Cheese

🕐 *PREP TIME: **15** MINUTES, COOK TIME: **10** MINUTES, SERVES: **8***

🍸 **INGREDIENTS:**
- 4 large zucchinis, sliced lengthwise into thin strips
- 8 ounces goat cheese, softened
- 2 tbsps. fresh basil, chopped
- 2 tbsps. fresh chives, chopped
- ¼ cup olive oil
- 2 cloves garlic, minced
- 2 tsps. kosher salt
- 2 tsps. black pepper
- Mesquite wood pellets

🍴 **DIRECTIONS:**
1. Preheat your Pit Boss Grill to 400°F.
2. In a small bowl, mix goat cheese, basil, and chives.
3. Spread a thin layer of the goat cheese mixture on each zucchini strip and roll them up.
4. Brush the zucchini rolls with olive oil, garlic, salt, and pepper.
5. Place the zucchini rolls on the grill.
6. Grill the zucchini rolls for about 5 minutes per side, until tender and slightly charred.
7. Serve warm.

Grilled Marinated Tofu Skewers

🕐 *PREP TIME: **20** MINUTES, PLUS **30** MINUTES FOR MARINATING, COOK TIME: **8** MINUTES, SERVES: **8***

🍸 **INGREDIENTS:**
- 2 blocks firm tofu, drained and cubed
- ¼ cup soy sauce
- 2 tbsps. rice vinegar
- 2 tbsps. olive oil
- 4 cloves garlic, minced
- 2 tbsps. fresh ginger, minced
- 2 tsps. sesame oil
- 2 tsps. black pepper
- 2 tsps. kosher salt
- Cherry wood pellets

🍳 **DIRECTIONS:**
1. Preheat your Pit Boss Grill to 450°F with the flame broiler open.
2. In a medium bowl, mix soy sauce, rice vinegar, olive oil, garlic, ginger, sesame oil, black pepper, and salt.
3. Marinate the tofu cubes in the mixture for at least 30 minutes.
4. Thread the marinated tofu onto skewers.
5. Grill the tofu skewers directly over the flame for about 3-4 minutes per side, until slightly charred.
6. Serve warm.

Buffalo Chicken Wings

🕐 *PREP TIME: **15** MINUTES, COOK TIME: **30** MINUTES, SERVES: **8***

🍸 **INGREDIENTS:**
- 4 pounds chicken wings
- ½ cup buffalo sauce
- 4 tbsps. olive oil
- 4 cloves garlic, minced
- 2 tbsps. smoked paprika
- 2 tsps. kosher salt
- 2 tsps. black pepper
- Hickory wood pellets

🍳 **DIRECTIONS:**
1. Preheat your Pit Boss Grill to 450°F with the flame broiler open.
2. In a large bowl, mix buffalo sauce, olive oil, garlic, smoked paprika, salt, and pepper.
3. Toss the chicken wings in the mixture to coat.
4. Place the chicken wings on the grill.
5. Grill the wings directly over the flame for about 15 minutes per side, until the internal temperature reaches 165°F and the skin is crispy.
6. Serve warm.

Grilled Pineapple Slices with Honey

🕐 *PREP TIME: **10** MINUTES, COOK TIME: **10** MINUTES, SERVES: **8***

🍸 **INGREDIENTS:**
- 1 pineapple, peeled, cored, and cut into rings
- ¼ cup honey
- 2 tbsps. lime juice
- 1 tsp. cinnamon
- 1 tsp. black pepper
- Mesquite wood pellets

🍳 **DIRECTIONS:**
1. Preheat your Pit Boss Grill to 450°F with the flame broiler open.
2. In a small bowl, mix honey, lime juice, cinnamon, and black pepper.
3. Brush the pineapple rings with the honey mixture.
4. Place the pineapple rings on the grill.
5. Grill the pineapple directly over the flame for about 5 minutes per side, until tender and slightly charred.
6. Serve warm.

Bacon-Wrapped Dates

🕐 *PREP TIME: **15** MINUTES, COOK TIME: **10** MINUTES, SERVES: **8***

🍸 **INGREDIENTS:**
- 24 large dates, pitted
- 12 slices bacon, halved
- 4 ounces blue cheese, crumbled
- 2 tbsps. honey
- 2 tsps. black pepper
- Pecan wood pellets

🍳 **DIRECTIONS:**
1. Preheat your Pit Boss Grill to 450°F with the flame broiler open.
2. Stuff each date with a small amount of blue cheese.
3. Wrap each stuffed date with a half slice of bacon and secure with a toothpick.
4. Place the bacon-wrapped dates on the grill.
5. Grill the dates directly over the flame for about 5 minutes per side, until the bacon is crispy.
6. Drizzle with honey and sprinkle with black pepper before serving. Serve warm.

Grilled Sausage and Cheese Platter

🕐 *PREP TIME: **10** MINUTES, COOK TIME: **15** MINUTES, SERVES: **8***

🏆 **INGREDIENTS:**
- 2 pounds assorted sausages
- ¼ cup olive oil
- 2 cloves garlic, minced
- 1 tsp. black pepper
- 1 tsp. kosher salt
- Assorted cheeses (such as cheddar, gouda, and brie)
- Assorted crackers
- Pecan wood pellets

🍴 **DIRECTIONS:**
1. Preheat your Pit Boss Grill to 450°F with the flame broiler open.
2. In a small bowl, mix olive oil, garlic, black pepper, and salt.
3. Brush the sausages with the olive oil mixture.
4. Place the sausages on the grill.
5. Grill the sausages directly over the flame for about 10-15 minutes, turning occasionally, until cooked through.
6. Serve the grilled sausages with assorted cheeses and crackers on a platter.

Cheese Stuffed Mushrooms

🕐 *PREP TIME: **15** MINUTES, COOK TIME: **16** MINUTES, SERVES: **6***

🏆 **INGREDIENTS:**
- 18 large white mushrooms, stems removed
- 6 ounces cream cheese, softened
- ¼ cup grated Parmesan cheese
- 6 cloves garlic, minced
- 2 tbsps. fresh parsley, chopped
- 2 tsps. black pepper
- 2 tsps. kosher salt
- Cherry wood pellets

🍴 **DIRECTIONS:**
1. Preheat your Pit Boss Grill to 400°F.
2. In a medium bowl, mix cream cheese, Parmesan cheese, garlic, parsley, black pepper, and salt.
3. Stuff each mushroom cap with the cream cheese mixture.
4. Place the stuffed mushrooms on the grill.
5. Grill the mushrooms for about 7-8 minutes per side, until the mushrooms are tender and the filling is melted and bubbly.
6. Serve warm.

Prosciutto-Wrapped Asparagus

🕐 *PREP TIME: **15** MINUTES, COOK TIME: **10** MINUTES, SERVES: **8***

🍴 **INGREDIENTS:**
- 32 asparagus spears, trimmed
- 16 slices prosciutto, halved lengthwise
- ¼ cup olive oil
- 2 cloves garlic, minced
- 2 tsps. lemon zest
- 2 tsps. black pepper
- 2 tsps. kosher salt
- Mesquite wood pellets

🍴 **DIRECTIONS:**
1. Preheat your Pit Boss Grill to 400°F.
2. In a small bowl, mix olive oil, garlic, lemon zest, black pepper, and salt.
3. Wrap each asparagus spear with a half slice of prosciutto.
4. Brush the prosciutto-wrapped asparagus with the olive oil mixture.
5. Place the asparagus on the grill.
6. Grill the asparagus for about 5 minutes per side, until the prosciutto is crispy and the asparagus is tender.
7. Serve warm.

Grilled Halloumi Cheese

🕐 *PREP TIME: **10** MINUTES, COOK TIME: **6** MINUTES, SERVES: **8***

🍴 **INGREDIENTS:**
- 16 ounces Halloumi cheese, sliced into ½-inch thick pieces
- ¼ cup olive oil
- 2 tbsps. lemon juice
- 2 cloves garlic, minced
- 2 tsps. dried oregano
- 2 tsps. black pepper
- Hickory wood pellets

🍴 **DIRECTIONS:**
1. Preheat your Pit Boss Grill to 450°F with the flame broiler open.
2. In a small bowl, mix olive oil, lemon juice, garlic, oregano, and black pepper.
3. Brush the Halloumi slices with the olive oil mixture.
4. Place the Halloumi slices on the grill.
5. Grill the Halloumi directly over the flame for about 2-3 minutes per side, until grill marks appear and the cheese is slightly charred.
6. Serve warm.

Garlic Parmesan Bread

🕐 *PREP TIME: **10** MINUTES, COOK TIME: **5** MINUTES, SERVES: **8***

🏆 **INGREDIENTS:**
- 1 large loaf French bread, sliced in half lengthwise
- ½ cup butter, melted
- 4 cloves garlic, minced
- 1 cup grated Parmesan cheese
- 2 tbsps. fresh parsley, chopped
- 1 tsp. black pepper
- Cherry wood pellets

🍽 **DIRECTIONS:**
1. Preheat your Pit Boss Grill to 450°F with the flame broiler open.
2. In a small bowl, mix melted butter, garlic, Parmesan cheese, parsley, and black pepper.
3. Brush the garlic Parmesan mixture onto the cut sides of the bread.
4. Place the bread halves on the grill, cut side down.
5. Grill the bread directly over the flame for about 5 minutes, until the bread is toasted and the cheese is melted.
6. Serve warm.

Cheese-Stuffed Mini Bell Peppers

🕐 *PREP TIME: **15** MINUTES, COOK TIME: **10** MINUTES, SERVES: **8***

🏆 **INGREDIENTS:**
- 24 mini bell peppers, halved and seeded
- 8 ounces cream cheese, softened
- 1 cup shredded mozzarella cheese
- 2 cloves garlic, minced
- 2 tsps. Italian seasoning
- 2 tsps. black pepper
- 2 tsps. kosher salt
- Cherry wood pellets

🍽 **DIRECTIONS:**
1. Preheat your Pit Boss Grill to 400°F.
2. In a medium bowl, mix cream cheese, mozzarella cheese, garlic, Italian seasoning, black pepper, and salt.
3. Stuff each mini bell pepper half with the cheese mixture.
4. Place the stuffed peppers on the grill.
5. Grill the peppers for about 5 minutes per side, until the peppers are tender and the cheese is melted and bubbly.
6. Serve warm.

Grilled Potato Skins

⏱ *PREP TIME: 20 MINUTES, COOK TIME: 20 MINUTES, SERVES: 8*

🍷 **INGREDIENTS:**

- 8 large russet potatoes
- ¼ cup olive oil
- 4 cloves garlic, minced
- 1 cup shredded cheddar cheese
- 8 slices bacon, cooked and crumbled
- ¼ cup sour cream
- 2 tbsps. fresh chives, chopped
- 2 tsps. black pepper
- 2 tsps. kosher salt
- Hickory wood pellets

♨ **DIRECTIONS:**

1. Preheat your Pit Boss Grill to 450°F with the flame broiler open.
2. Pierce the potatoes with a fork and microwave for 5-6 minutes, until slightly softened. Let cool, then slice each potato in half lengthwise and scoop out some of the flesh, leaving a ¼-inch thick shell.
3. In a small bowl, mix olive oil, garlic, black pepper, and salt. Brush the potato skins with the mixture.
4. Place the potato skins on the grill, cut side down.
5. Grill the potato skins directly over the flame for about 10 minutes, until crispy.
6. Flip the potato skins and fill each with cheddar cheese and bacon.
7. Grill for an additional 5 minutes, until the cheese is melted.
8. Top each potato skin with a dollop of sour cream and a sprinkle of chives. Serve warm.

Spicy Shrimp Tacos

⏱ *PREP TIME: 20 MINUTES, COOK TIME: 6 MINUTES, SERVES: 8*

🍷 **INGREDIENTS:**

- 2 pounds large shrimp, peeled and deveined
- ¼ cup olive oil
- 4 cloves garlic, minced
- 2 tbsps. lime juice
- 2 tbsps. fresh cilantro, chopped
- 2 tsps. chili powder
- 2 tsps. cumin
- 2 tsps. kosher salt
- 2 tsps. black pepper
- 16 small corn tortillas
- 2 cups shredded cabbage
- 1 cup salsa
- 1 cup sour cream
- Apple wood pellets

♨ **DIRECTIONS:**

1. Preheat your Pit Boss Grill to 450°F with the flame broiler open.
2. In a large bowl, mix olive oil, garlic, lime juice, cilantro, chili powder, cumin, salt, and pepper.
3. Toss the shrimp in the mixture to coat.
4. Thread the shrimp onto skewers.
5. Grill the shrimp skewers directly over the flame for about 2-3 minutes per side, until the shrimp are opaque and cooked through.
6. Serve the grilled shrimp in tortillas with shredded cabbage, salsa, and sour cream.

Chapter 9: Baking and Desserts

Rosemary Dinner Rolls

⏱ PREP TIME: **20** MINUTES, PLUS **1** HOUR FOR RISING, COOK TIME: **20** MINUTES, SERVES: **8**

🏆 **INGREDIENTS:**
- 1 package active dry yeast
- 1 cup warm water
- 2 tbsps. sugar
- 1 tsp. salt
- 2 tbsps. olive oil
- 3 cups all-purpose flour
- 2 tbsps. fresh rosemary, chopped

🍴 **DIRECTIONS:**
1. Preheat your Pit Boss Grill to 350°F.
2. In a large bowl, dissolve the yeast in warm water. Add sugar, salt, olive oil, and 1 cup flour. Beat until smooth.
3. Stir in enough remaining flour to form a soft dough.
4. Knead on a floured surface for about 5 minutes, until smooth and elastic.
5. Place the dough in a greased bowl, cover, and let rise until doubled, about 1 hour.
6. Punch down the dough and divide into 12 pieces. Shape into balls and place in a greased baking dish.
7. Sprinkle the top with chopped rosemary.
8. Place the baking dish on the grill.
9. Bake for about 20 minutes, until the rolls are golden brown.
10. Serve warm.

Blueberry Lemon Bread

⏱ PREP TIME: **15** MINUTES, COOK TIME: **1** HOUR, SERVES: **8**

🏆 **INGREDIENTS:**
- ½ cup butter, softened
- 1 cup sugar
- 2 eggs
- 1 tbsp. lemon zest
- 1 tbsp. lemon juice
- 1½ cups flour
- 1 tsp. baking powder
- ½ tsp. salt
- ½ cup milk
- 1 cup fresh blueberries

🍴 **DIRECTIONS:**
1. Preheat your Pit Boss Grill to 350°F.
2. In a large bowl, cream the butter and sugar until light and fluffy.
3. Beat in the eggs, lemon zest, and lemon juice.
4. In another bowl, whisk together the flour, baking powder, and salt.
5. Gradually add the dry ingredients to the wet ingredients, alternating with the milk, mixing until just combined.
6. Gently fold in the blueberries.
7. Pour the batter into a greased loaf pan.
8. Place the loaf pan on the grill.
9. Bake for about 1 hour, until a toothpick inserted into the center comes out clean.
10. Let the bread cool in the pan for 10 minutes before transferring to a wire rack to cool completely. Serve warm or at room temperature.

Cinnamon Sugar Donuts

*PREP TIME: **20** MINUTES, COOK TIME: **15** MINUTES, SERVES: **8***

INGREDIENTS:
- 2 cups all-purpose flour
- ½ cup sugar
- 2 tsps. baking powder
- ½ tsp. salt
- ½ tsp. ground cinnamon
- ¼ tsp. ground nutmeg
- ½ cup milk
- ¼ cup butter, melted
- 2 eggs
- 1 tsp. vanilla extract
- 1 cup sugar
- 1 tbsp. ground cinnamon
- ¼ cup butter, melted

DIRECTIONS:
1. Preheat your Pit Boss Grill to 350°F.
2. In a large bowl, whisk together flour, ½ cup sugar, baking powder, salt, ½ tsp. ground cinnamon, and ground nutmeg.
3. In another bowl, mix milk, ¼ cup melted butter, eggs, and vanilla extract.
4. Gradually add the wet ingredients to the dry ingredients, mixing until just combined.
5. Pour the batter into a greased donut pan.
6. Place the donut pan on the grill.
7. Bake for about 15 minutes, until the donuts are golden brown and a toothpick inserted into the center comes out clean.
8. In a small bowl, mix 1 cup sugar and 1 tbsp. ground cinnamon.
9. Brush the warm donuts with melted butter and dip in the cinnamon sugar mixture. Serve warm.

Apple Pie

*PREP TIME: **30** MINUTES, COOK TIME: **1** HOUR, SERVES: **8***

INGREDIENTS:
- 6 large apples, peeled, cored, and sliced
- 1 cup sugar
- ½ cup brown sugar
- 1 tsp. cinnamon
- ¼ tsp. nutmeg
- ¼ tsp. allspice
- 2 tbsps. flour
- 2 tbsps. lemon juice
- 2 pie crusts

DIRECTIONS:
1. Preheat your Pit Boss Grill to 350°F.
2. In a large bowl, mix the apples, sugar, brown sugar, cinnamon, nutmeg, allspice, flour, and lemon juice.
3. Line a baking dish with one pie crust and fill with the apple mixture.
4. Cover with the second pie crust, sealing the edges.
5. Place the baking dish on the grill.
6. Bake for about 1 hour, until the crust is golden brown and the filling is bubbly.
7. Serve warm.

Cheddar Biscuits

🕐 *PREP TIME: **15** MINUTES, COOK TIME: **20** MINUTES, SERVES: **8***

🍷 **INGREDIENTS:**
- 2 cups all-purpose flour
- 1 tbsp. baking powder
- ½ tsp. baking soda
- ½ tsp. salt
- ½ cup cold butter, cubed
- 1 cup shredded cheddar cheese
- 1 cup buttermilk

🍳 **DIRECTIONS:**
1. Preheat your Pit Boss Grill to 350°F.
2. In a large bowl, whisk together flour, baking powder, baking soda, and salt.
3. Cut in the cold butter until the mixture resembles coarse crumbs.
4. Stir in the shredded cheddar cheese.
5. Add the buttermilk and mix until just combined.
6. Drop spoonfuls of the dough onto a baking sheet.
7. Place the baking sheet on the grill.
8. Bake for about 20 minutes, until the biscuits are golden brown.
9. Serve warm.

Three-Cheese Macaroni

🕐 *PREP TIME: **20** MINUTES, COOK TIME: **32** MINUTES, SERVES: **8***

🍷 **INGREDIENTS:**
- 1 pound elbow macaroni
- ¼ cup butter
- ¼ cup all-purpose flour
- 3 cups milk
- 1 cup shredded cheddar cheese
- 1 cup shredded mozzarella cheese
- 1 cup shredded Parmesan cheese
- ½ tsp. salt
- ½ tsp. black pepper

🍳 **DIRECTIONS:**
1. Preheat your Pit Boss Grill to 350°F.
2. Cook the macaroni according to the package instructions. Drain and set aside.
3. In a large saucepan, melt the butter over medium heat. Stir in the flour and cook for 1-2 minutes, until bubbly.
4. Gradually whisk in the milk and cook, stirring constantly, until the mixture thickens.
5. Stir in the cheddar cheese, mozzarella cheese, Parmesan cheese, salt, and black pepper until the cheese is melted and the sauce is smooth.
6. Add the cooked macaroni to the cheese sauce and stir until well combined.
7. Pour the mixture into a greased baking dish.
8. Place the baking dish on the grill.
9. Bake for about 30 minutes, until the top is golden brown and the macaroni is heated through.
10. Serve warm.

Herb Focaccia

🕐 *PREP TIME: **20** MINUTES, PLUS **1** HOUR FOR RISING, COOK TIME: **25** MINUTES, SERVES: **8***

🍸 **INGREDIENTS:**
- 2¼ tsps. active dry yeast
- 1½ cups warm water
- 3½ cups all-purpose flour
- ¼ cup olive oil
- 2 tsps. salt
- 2 tbsps. fresh rosemary, chopped
- 2 tbsps. fresh thyme, chopped

🍳 **DIRECTIONS:**
1. Preheat your Pit Boss Grill to 400°F.
2. In a large bowl, dissolve the yeast in warm water. Let sit for 5 minutes, until frothy.
3. Add the flour, olive oil, and salt to the yeast mixture. Mix until a dough forms.
4. Knead the dough on a floured surface for about 5 minutes, until smooth and elastic.
5. Place the dough in a greased bowl, cover, and let rise for 1 hour, until doubled in size.
6. Punch down the dough and press it into a greased baking pan.
7. Brush the top with olive oil and sprinkle with chopped rosemary and thyme.
8. Place the baking pan on the grill.
9. Bake for about 25 minutes, until golden brown.
10. Serve warm.

Gouda and Spinach Quiche

🕐 *PREP TIME: **20** MINUTES, COOK TIME: **47** MINUTES, SERVES: **8***

🍸 **INGREDIENTS:**
- 1 pie crust
- 1 tbsp. olive oil
- 1 small onion, chopped
- 2 cups fresh spinach, chopped
- 1 cup shredded gouda cheese
- 4 eggs
- 1 cup milk
- ½ tsp. salt
- ½ tsp. black pepper

🍳 **DIRECTIONS:**
1. Preheat your Pit Boss Grill to 350°F.
2. In a skillet, heat the olive oil over medium heat. Add the chopped onion and cook until softened, about 5 minutes.
3. Add the chopped spinach and cook until wilted, about 2 minutes.
4. Place the pie crust in a greased pie dish.
5. Spread the cooked onion and spinach mixture over the pie crust.
6. Sprinkle the shredded gouda cheese over the vegetables.
7. In a bowl, whisk together the eggs, milk, salt, and black pepper. Pour over the cheese and vegetables in the pie crust.
8. Place the pie dish on the grill.
9. Bake for about 40 minutes, until the quiche is set and the top is golden brown.
10. Serve warm.

Parmesan Garlic Knots

*PREP TIME: **20** MINUTES, COOK TIME: **20** MINUTES, SERVES: **8***

INGREDIENTS:
- 1 can refrigerated pizza dough
- ¼ cup butter, melted
- 4 cloves garlic, minced
- ¼ cup grated Parmesan cheese
- 2 tbsps. fresh parsley, chopped

DIRECTIONS:
1. Preheat your Pit Boss Grill to 350°F.
2. Roll out the pizza dough and cut into strips.
3. Tie each strip into a knot and place on a greased baking sheet.
4. In a small bowl, mix melted butter and minced garlic.
5. Brush the garlic butter over the dough knots.
6. Place the baking sheet on the grill.
7. Bake for about 15-20 minutes, until the knots are golden brown.
8. Sprinkle with grated Parmesan cheese and chopped parsley before serving. Serve warm.

Jalapeño Cornbread

*PREP TIME: **15** MINUTES, COOK TIME: **25** MINUTES, SERVES: **8***

INGREDIENTS:
- 1 cup cornmeal
- 1 cup all-purpose flour
- ¼ cup sugar
- 1 tbsp. baking powder
- ½ tsp. salt
- 1 cup milk
- ¼ cup vegetable oil
- 2 eggs
- 1 cup shredded cheddar cheese
- ½ cup diced jalapeños

DIRECTIONS:
1. Preheat your Pit Boss Grill to 400°F.
2. In a large bowl, whisk together cornmeal, flour, sugar, baking powder, and salt.
3. In another bowl, mix milk, vegetable oil, and eggs.
4. Gradually add the wet ingredients to the dry ingredients, mixing until just combined.
5. Stir in the shredded cheddar cheese and diced jalapeños.
6. Pour the batter into a greased baking dish.
7. Place the baking dish on the grill.
8. Bake for about 25 minutes, until the top is golden brown and a toothpick inserted into the center comes out clean.
9. Serve warm.

Lemon Bars

🕐 *PREP TIME:* **20** *MINUTES, COOK TIME:* **35** *MINUTES, SERVES:* **12**

🍸 INGREDIENTS:

- 1 cup butter, softened
- 2 cups all-purpose flour
- ½ cup powdered sugar
- 4 large eggs
- 2 cups granulated sugar
- ¼ cup all-purpose flour
- ½ cup lemon juice
- 1 tbsp. lemon zest
- Powdered sugar for dusting
- Apple wood pellets

🍳 DIRECTIONS:

1. Preheat your Pit Boss Grill to 350°F.
2. In a large bowl, mix the softened butter, 2 cups flour, and ½ cup powdered sugar until a dough forms.
3. Press the dough into a greased 9x13-inch baking dish.
4. Place the baking dish on the grill.
5. Bake for about 15-20 minutes, until the crust is golden brown.
6. In another bowl, whisk together the eggs, granulated sugar, ¼ cup flour, lemon juice, and lemon zest until well combined.
7. Pour the lemon mixture over the baked crust.
8. Place the baking dish back on the grill.
9. Bake for about 15-20 minutes, until the lemon filling is set.
10. Let the lemon bars cool completely before dusting with powdered sugar and slicing. Serve chilled or at room temperature.

Peach Cobbler

🕐 *PREP TIME:* **20** *MINUTES, COOK TIME:* **30** *MINUTES, SERVES:* **8**

🍸 INGREDIENTS:

- 5 large peaches, sliced
- 1 cup sugar
- ½ cup brown sugar
- ¼ cup butter, melted
- 1 tsp. cinnamon
- 1 cup flour
- 1 cup milk
- 2 tsps. baking powder

🍳 DIRECTIONS:

1. Preheat your Pit Boss Grill to 350°F.
2. In a large bowl, mix the peaches, ½ cup sugar, brown sugar, and cinnamon.
3. In another bowl, mix the flour, ½ cup sugar, milk, baking powder, and melted butter.
4. Pour the peach mixture into a casserole dish, then pour the batter over the peaches.
5. Place the casserole dish on the grill.
6. Bake for about 30 minutes, until the top is golden brown and the peaches are bubbly.
7. Serve warm.

Appendix 1:
Basic Kitchen Conversions & Equivalents

DRY MEASUREMENTS CONVERSION CHART

3 teaspoons = 1 tablespoon = 1/16 cup
6 teaspoons = 2 tablespoons = 1/8 cup
12 teaspoons = 4 tablespoons = ¼ cup
24 teaspoons = 8 tablespoons = ½ cup
36 teaspoons = 12 tablespoons = ¾ cup
48 teaspoons = 16 tablespoons = 1 cup

METRIC TO US COOKING CONVERSIONS

OVEN TEMPERATURES
120 °C = 250 °F
160 °C = 320 °F
180 °C = 350 °F
205 °C = 400 °F
220 °C = 425 °F

LIQUID MEASUREMENTS CONVERSION CHART
8 fluid ounces = 1 cup = ½ pint = ¼ quart
16 fluid ounces = 2 cups = 1 pint = ½ quart
32 fluid ounces = 4 cups = 2 pints = 1 quart = ¼ gallon
128 fluid ounces = 16 cups = 8 pints = 4 quarts = 1 gallon

BAKING IN GRAMS
1 cup flour = 140 grams
1 cup sugar = 150 grams
1 cup powdered sugar = 160 grams
1 cup heavy cream = 235 grams

VOLUME
1 milliliter = 1/5 teaspoon
5 ml = 1 teaspoon
15 ml = 1 tablespoon
240 ml = 1 cup or 8 fluid ounces
1 liter = 34 fluid ounces

WEIGHT
1 gram = .035 ounces
100 grams = 3.5 ounces
500 grams = 1.1 pounds
1 kilogram = 35 ounces

US TO METRIC COOKING CONVERSIONS

1/5 tsp = 1 ml
1 tsp = 5 ml
1 tbsp = 15 ml
1 fluid ounces = 30 ml
1 cup = 237 ml
1 pint (2 cups) = 473 ml
1 quart (4 cups) = .95 liter
1 gallon (16 cups) = 3.8 liters
1 oz = 28 grams
1 pound = 454 grams

BUTTER
1 cup butter = 2 sticks = 8 ounces = 230 grams = 16 tablespoons

WHAT DOES 1 CUP EQUAL
1 cup = 8 fluid ounces
1 cup = 16 tablespoons
1 cup = 48 teaspoons
1 cup = ½ pint
1 cup = ¼ quart
1 cup = 1/16 gallon
1 cup = 240 ml

BAKING PAN CONVERSIONS
9-inch round cake pan = 12 cups
10-inch tube pan =16 cups
10-inch bundt pan = 12 cups
9-inch springform pan = 10 cups
9 x 5 inch loaf pan = 8 cups
9-inch square pan = 8 cups

BAKING PAN CONVERSIONS
1 cup all-purpose flour = 4.5 oz
1 cup rolled oats = 3 oz
1 large egg = 1.7 oz
1 cup butter = 8 oz
1 cup milk = 8 oz
1 cup heavy cream = 8.4 oz
1 cup granulated sugar = 7.1 oz
1 cup packed brown sugar = 7.75 oz
1 cup vegetable oil = 7.7 oz
1 cup unsifted powdered sugar = 4.4 oz

Appendix 2: Recipes Index

HERE ARE YOUR FREE BONUSES:

PIT BOSS WOOD PELLET
GRILL & SMOKER USER MANUAL

SAUCES & SPICY RUB RECIPES

PAPERBACK PDF

STEP 1: POST A QUICK REVIEW

Qualify to receive the 3 free Bonuses by posting a SUPER QUICK review on
AMAZON.COM (Optional, but I'd really love to get your Feedback)

POST A REVIEW

STEP 2: GET YOUR QUALIFY
Send your review record to me by scanning
QR CODE

STEP 3: DOWNLOAD YOUR FREE BONUSES

Now you can download your BONUSES

USER MANUAL

SAUCES & SPICEY RUB RECIPE

PAPERBACK PDF

Made in United States
Orlando, FL
14 December 2024

55650155R30043